PRINCIPLE-BASED
LEADERSHIP

PRINCIPLE-BASED
LEADERSHIP

DRIVING YOUR SUCCESS AS A LEADER

JIM ANDERSON

iUniverse LLC
Bloomington

PRINCIPLE-BASED LEADERSHIP
Driving Your Success as a Leader

iUniverse books may be ordered through booksellers or by contacting:

iUniverse LLC
1663 Liberty Drive
Bloomington, IN 47403
www.iuniverse.com
1-800-Authors (1-800-288-4677)

Because of the dynamic nature of the Internet, any web addresses or links contained in this book may have changed since publication and may no longer be valid. The views expressed in this work are solely those of the author and do not necessarily reflect the views of the publisher, and the publisher hereby disclaims any responsibility for them.

Any people depicted in stock imagery provided by Thinkstock are models, and such images are being used for illustrative purposes only.
Certain stock imagery © Thinkstock.

ISBN: 978-1-4917-0034-1 (sc)
ISBN: 978-1-4917-0036-5 (hc)
ISBN: 978-1-4917-0035-8 (e)

Library of Congress Control Number: 2013913889

Printed in the United States of America

iUniverse rev. date: 01/15/2014

CONTENTS

In memory of Richard G. Mohn:
a living lesson in principle-based leadership

FOREWORD

Thirty years after launching a business that became an international company, twenty after beginning to invest and build other businesses, and ten after founding my current one, some core questions still persist—How can *I* be a better leader? Where can I find *others* with strong leadership? How can I *encourage others* to be more effective leaders? As a business psychologist having grown global human resources consulting and hiring businesses to serve most of the Fortune 100, these questions never stop surfacing . . . and the answers keep evolving.

In *finding leaders*, there is lots of "science" that helps decide what to look for. But as the head of a business that needs to *be a leader as well as encourage leadership in others*, there are times I see the science of finding leaders is only part of the challenge. This is where I've found the concepts, principles, and tools presented in **Principle-Based Leadership** play a major role in growing and encouraging leadership at all levels of organizations.

Statistics tell us roughly 60 percent of newly hired leaders in business fail within a few years after taking the position. At the higher levels of an organization, the cost of such failures runs in the millions—lost opportunity, termination, next-stage recruiting costs, and the price paid for lowered engagement among the failed leader's team and employees. Because organizations are only as successful as those who lead them, many today invest much time and resources in finding, developing, and attempting to build effective leaders at all levels. **Principle-Based Leadership** can be a valuable tool in this mission.

Experience tells us something more . . . every leader and team member comes to the workplace with 'Can Do' and 'Will Do' qualities. The more organizations and leaders encourage the

'Will Do' to take center stage . . . and grow such competencies, as described in *Principle-Based Leadership*, the more likely they will build outstanding leaders and achieve success.

Principle-Based Leadership serves as a complete self-help program for individuals who want to become better leaders, as well as an excellent learning tool for organizations who wish to promote strong leadership within their ranks at all levels. Because it provides numerous practical assessment and goal setting exercises with case studies it is unexcelled for ensuring readers *will use what they learn*.

How do I know the practical concepts described in *Principle-Based Leadership* help those who want to be better leaders . . . and those who want to find and develop leaders? I have firsthand experience when Jim Anderson carried the concepts into my organization, helped me apply them, and delivered leadership development for my senior-most leaders. And when you are busy growing a business, the more practical, understandable, and actionable the ideas presented, the better. That's what I've experienced working with Jim. The concepts he presents in *Principle-Based Leadership* will provide you the same benefits.

In my experience, practical "know how" drives leadership success. *Principle-Based Leadership* helps a leader know what to do when a team member misses a target and needs redirection, strays off course and needs constructive feedback, or when a superior asks for something that just does not make sense and needs to be told why in a manner they will understand.

Jim Anderson has laid out the best recipe for *becoming* an effective leader or *building leadership* in your organization that I have seen. The real world knowledge offered here can help leaders at all age and experience levels to achieve outstanding success. If you turn the page, the reasons this book will have such value for you will start to emerge.

David P Jones, PhD
President & CEO
Growth Ventures, Inc.

PREFACE

The greater a person's ability to lead, the more success they will have, in all aspects of their life. This is particularly true in pursuits that involve interacting or working closely with others. While there are countless books, articles, and resources on leadership, it's not always easy to apply their lessons in the real world. After coaching hundreds of successful leaders and professionals, I have written this book to relate what I have learned about leadership from them and also to describe how the reader may apply the information in practice.

For the past thirty-five years, I have served as an executive coach and management consultant to Fortune 500 companies and public sector organizations; this experience has revealed to me many essential qualities and necessary skills of outstanding leaders. Unquestionably, one of the most essential attributes of effective leaders is that they create positive outcomes for those they lead. They improve the lives of others. They achieve this end because they place a high priority upon the interests of others, often above their own. They seek to serve. This is a function of the principles by which they are guided.

Learning to lead more effectively is a never ending process. No matter how experienced you are at leading, you can always become better. This book addresses three interwoven components that can strengthen your ability to lead, regardless of the level of your current leadership skill. One component describes essential leadership *qualities and practices,* with emphasis upon highly regarded principles at the core. The second provides *assessment tools and exercises* that will enable you to better capitalize on your natural leadership abilities and develop them in others. The third addresses *how to apply what you learn* to your current leadership position or your life beyond formal roles.

I have chosen to place my primary focus upon the variable that in my experience provides the best foundation for a leader's success: principle-based leadership. Principles are not a new topic when discussing effective leadership. Many credible leadership experts propose that demonstrating principles is essential for building genuine respect as well as commitment when working directly with or influencing others. However, my focus will go beyond highlighting the importance of principles to actually using them as a guideline for *what to do* to lead more effectively.

Principle-based leadership is largely about service. For leaders to be truly effective, their influence must result in leading others to desirable or constructive outcomes. There can be no more service-based function than that. Principle-based leadership is demonstrated through character and values in the leader that others respect. While values and norms of behavior may vary across cultures, some are universally embraced in most contexts. Such values include integrity, selflessness, caring, and courage.

Many of the leadership lessons and tools in this book promote experiential learning as well as direct application. This approach provides an opportunity to study a technique and then apply it in your current role; the same approach has contributed to the success of many of the outstanding leaders described herein. Additionally, the principles that made these leaders effective are illustrated through several of their life experiences.

The men and women I have chosen for study illustrate outstanding leadership qualities and skills; they have a common keystone in their leadership profile. That keystone is *integrity*. While that may sound like it should be a given for leaders, too frequently it is not. Integrity is not often found among today's leaders, just as it was frequently missing from those who held significant leadership positions throughout history.

By integrity, I refer to the act of placing honesty at the core of how you lead. It means you are trustworthy, fulfill your promises, and meet commitments. Leaders with integrity can be depended on to do what they say. I will examine the advantages of principle-based leadership, centered upon integrity and its unsurpassed utility for establishing the level of trust and influence that encourages the best in others. I will also examine the critical importance of developing excellent decision skills, achieving competence in your area of responsibility, and displaying effective human relations skills.

This book was initiated as a result of my work through the Greenbrier Leadership Institute, a nonprofit educational organization. The institute develops and delivers a variety of live leadership programs as well as educational products and services for the public. All revenues from the sale of this book are passed along to the institute to help sustain its public service efforts. It also serves as the primary text that supports the institute's programs.

All that is presented here is done so as an *integrated whole*. To obtain the full value of what will be covered, it is necessary to do more than just read the chapters. Beyond studying the skills, attributes, and techniques of outstanding leaders, you will be given exercises to strengthen your ability to lead. Case studies with questions and answers are used to further facilitate learning. You will be referred at various points to GreenbrierLeadership.com to access assessments and exercises matched to specific chapters. Skipping around to different sections that may appear to be of most interest will most likely undermine the value of the program.

Regardless of your age, role, or existing leadership abilities and experience, if you invest the time and effort required to complete the work and finish the full program, you will strengthen your ability to lead. This in turn will increase your success at almost any endeavor that involves interacting with, managing, or working with others.

ACKNOWLEDGMENTS

I am very grateful not only for the support and encouragement from so many people while I was writing this book, but also for their excellent counsel and advice on the project at each step. The support came from professional associates, educators, clients, friends, and family, who all brought a wealth of leadership experience to the process.

Colonel W. Beaman Cummings, USMC (Ret.), my partner in founding the Greenbrier Leadership Institute in 2008, contributed countless hours of editing and counsel. Additionally, he has served in a central role in garnering support for the Greenbrier Leadership Institute, without which this book would not have been written. Colonel Cummings and I also owe a debt of gratitude to John Curry, the former superintendent of the Greenbrier County Schools, who suggested a formal organization that ultimately led to the creation of the institute.

Colonel Lee Martin, US Army (Ret.), has been instrumental in bringing this book to life. His original encouragement of my activities through the Greenbrier Military School Alumni Association (GMSAA), the parent of the Greenbrier Leadership Institute, was the direct source of inspiration for all we are doing through the institute today. Lee has also contributed enormously to the editing of the manuscript.

Herb Pearis, the secretary of the GMSAA, kept the parent organization alive and vital for most of the years after the school closed in 1972. This ultimately provided the platform for the formation of the institute. Herb and Phil McLaughlin, the treasurer of the Alumni Association, made possible much of what we are doing now through the Institute, including publishing this book.

Grey Webb, the president of the GMSAA, and other supporters within the association, have greatly facilitated the Greenbrier Leadership Institute. While there are too many to name here, a number of GMSAA members have been instrumental in ensuring that the legacy of Greenbrier Military School is furthered through the institute. A few of the more prominent members are Bill Isbister, Calvin Garvin, James Roberts, John Byrnes, Mike Lee, Jim Justice, John Schneider, and Admiral Ted Parker, USN (Ret.)

Additionally, invaluable editing advice, personal perspectives, and insightful content suggestions were provided by Cathy Christiansen, Lauren Douglas, and Alyssa Christiansen.

CHAPTER 1
DEFINING LEADERSHIP

The elderly janitor stepped aside as the group of young cadets hustled down the hall to their classrooms. The old man, known only as "Bill" to the Air Force Academy cadets, was shy and unassuming in his role as the squadron janitor and kept to himself. He typically did not speak unless someone spoke to him. He was only known for years at the academy by most for the excellent job he did keeping the barracks spotless. Hardly anyone paid attention to Bill as he served in his role with quiet dignity.

However, Bill's role changed significantly on a fall afternoon in 1976 when a young cadet by the name of James Moschgat was studying about an important battle in World War II and learned of an American soldier, Private William Crawford. Moschgat read how Private Crawford had demonstrated heroic leadership and set an example of courage for his platoon members while performing valiant feats of bravery.

His actions earned him the Medal of Honor, the military's highest award, for his service in Italy in September of 1943. Cadet Moschgat discovered how Crawford, on his own initiative, courageously and single-handedly attacked enemy machine gun nests that were holding back the advance of his platoon. In doing so, he saved the lives of many of his fellow platoon members.

Years later, Colonel James Moschgat, USAF (Ret.), wrote:

> I said to my roommate, "You're not going to believe this but I think our janitor is a Medal of Honor winner." We all knew Mr. Crawford was a WWII Army vet, but that didn't keep my friend from looking at me as if I was some sort of alien

being. Nonetheless we couldn't wait to ask Bill about the story on Monday morning. We met Mr. Crawford bright and early Monday and showed him the page in question from the book, anticipation and doubt in our faces. He stared at it for a few silent moments and then quietly uttered something like, "Yep, that's me." Mouths agape, my roommate and I looked at one another, then at the book, and quickly back at our janitor. Almost at once we both stuttered, "Why didn't you ever tell us about it?" He slowly replied after some thought, "That was one day in my life, and it happened a long time ago." I guess we were all at a loss for words after that.[1]

But from that moment on, as word spread about his heroism in World War II, Bill Crawford assumed a new role with the cadets at the Air Force Academy. Though he had said nothing to promote himself, the mere awareness of his actions so many years before instantly changed the cadets' perspective about him. He was no longer "just a janitor." Quickly cadets began to refer to him as "Mr. Crawford." And soon many cadets began to seek his perspective upon personal issues and academy matters. He was invited to functions and sought after for his insight upon various subjects important to cadets at all levels. Through soft-spoken counsel and encouragement of those cadets who began to seek his advice, Bill became a valued informal leader at the academy.

But although Bill assumed a new role of leadership for the cadets, he continued to maintain his modest persona and serve in a humble manner, fulfilling his janitorial duties as before. And what many cadets learned from Bill was a lesson about leadership that would never leave them: the nature of true leadership is *service* to others above all and is demonstrated not by words but by actions.

What Exactly Is Leadership?

Almost everyone is provided an opportunity to lead at one time or another. The opportunity may occur in a formal role, such as heading a business, a club, or a team. It may arise informally within a gathering of friends, in a family, or during an unexpected crisis. Regardless, leadership opportunities occur wherever two or more people gather. For people to accomplish anything productive together, a direction must be established, and whoever establishes that direction leads. But leadership roles vary greatly.

The specific leadership responsibilities for a naval captain on an aircraft carrier are certainly very different from that of an executive director of a policy institute that researches technology issues. However, both roles share similar requirements in that they must establish direction, solve problems, and work through other people. And all leaders must *influence others* toward necessary actions.[2]

The naval captain and the executive director also share important responsibilities such as encouraging excellent performance of individuals, leading teams, and guiding the organization they head. So, while leadership roles may have very different contexts and expected outcomes, they all share core requirements that are essential if the leader is to be effective.

The most essential requirement of leadership is that to be truly effective, *leaders must lead*. They must find constructive paths toward success. And that is not often easy. By lead, I am referring to the action that *provides direction* to others that will ultimately yield beneficial results for those who are led and those who they, in turn, may influence.

> *For people to accomplish anything productive together, a direction must be established, and whoever establishes that direction leads.*

Leadership may be performed formally by someone with authority, such as a chief executive officer of a business, or informally by a member of a project team who offers valuable and practical suggestions that benefit the team. If members of that team accept and commit to using the suggestions of the team member who offered them, he or she is demonstrating leadership through their influence, even without formal authority.

Ultimately, effective leadership is the ability to set and promote positive direction for others and gain their commitment to follow. The term "positive direction" is paramount. If leaders set paths toward failure or harmful outcomes, regardless of how popular or widely respected in the interim, they are not successful leaders.

It is important to emphasize that formal authority alone does not make the leader. People are not necessarily willing to follow anyone just because of authority. They might comply with formal orders or tasks assigned to avoid negative consequences; however, that does not mean they are either eager or willing. To gain the willingness of others to follow, effective leaders must influence others toward something they believe is worthwhile. There must be genuine commitment to the leader's direction. And that often has much more to do with how they *feel* about the leader than what their role is.

Why Is Genuine Commitment of Followers so Important to Be an Effective Leader?

The Revolutionary War found the Continental army troops, under the command of General George Washington, almost hopelessly outnumbered. They were underequipped and poorly trained. Possibly the lowest point in the entire campaign was the winter of 1777-78. At that point, what remained of the troops was camped at Valley Forge in Pennsylvania. Fewer than half the troops had shoes, and the rest hobbled around in the snow with their feet wrapped in rags.[3]

> *Effective leadership is the ability to set and promote positive direction for others and gain their commitment to follow.*

A significant portion of the 12,500 troops had pneumonia, typhoid, dysentery, or jaundice. They had so little to eat that boot leather and horse meat became commonplace as nourishment. Before the winter ended, over 2,500 of the men died from disease. But the majority of those who survived remained committed. Why?

The soldiers' willingness to remain was based upon the deep respect they had for the cause their leader represented. But George Washington not only *represented* the cause of liberty and independence for which they fought, he *demonstrated* the same dedication they did. He was one of those rare commanders who did not direct his forces safely from afar; he actually fought side by side with them. He led on the front lines. He was routinely observed commanding from horseback in the midst of exploding shells and deadly hails of musket balls. Washington appealed to the basic nature of what drives humans to be willing to sacrifice all in the interest of a worthy cause.

> *High sentiments always win in the end; the leaders who offer blood, toil, tears, and sweat always get more out of their followers than those who offer safety and a good time. When it comes to the pinch, human beings are heroic.*[4]—George Orwell

While Washington's leadership at Valley Forge is an extreme case of how a leader gains the willingness of followers to commit, the principle illustrated is essentially the same, regardless of the leadership context. Effective leaders gain a commitment that exceeds simple compliance. And this is why they achieve outstanding results. Deep commitment to anything is driven more by how people *feel* than what they think about the cause.

> *Mankind are governed more by their feelings than by reason.*—Samuel Adams

Is There an Absolute Formula for Building Commitment?

Not exactly. But there are a number of skills and qualities that are commonly shared by effective leaders, regardless of context, that promote commitment. The circumstances that Agnes Gonxha Bojaxhiu, more commonly known as Mother Teresa, faced were very different from those George Washington faced. She did not lead people in a life-or-death struggle,

> *The nature of true leadership is service to others above all and is demonstrated not by words but by actions.*

yet she gained enormous commitment from followers who were willing to devote their lives wholeheartedly to missionary work in poverty-stricken and oftentimes dangerous conditions.

Mother Teresa and her followers began by ministering to the poor, sick, orphaned, and dying in the squalid back streets of Calcutta. Over the next forty-five years, throughout India and ultimately worldwide, they served millions. She would not have been able to achieve such a level of commitment if she did not represent a cause that instilled a sense of great purpose and meaning to her followers. The commitment she earned was not a function of what she said but a function of her deeds and the cause she embodied. Her actions evoked far more influence than her words ever could have.

Building commitment is a necessity for effective leadership in all contexts. Whether running a business, serving in politics, working in a nonprofit setting, or even athletic coaching, if leaders cannot establish commitment that lasts throughout difficult circumstances, they will ultimately fail.

Athletic coaches often demonstrate the kinds of leadership challenges common in great endeavors. All athletic teams and their head coaches, regardless how strong, will experience disappointing setbacks. Tony Dungy, the Super Bowl—winning coach of the Indianapolis Colts, has become one of the best examples of the unusual fortitude that must sometimes be displayed to be a successful leader in a coaching role. Coach Dungy demonstrated well what leaders must do to build deep commitment that both bolsters and sustains their teams during the most difficult trials.

Dungy took over as head coach of the Colts in 2002; his team's road to a Super Bowl victory in the 2006-7 season was beset by numerous heart-breaking setbacks. But the lowest and most severe point for Coach Dungy occurred in 2005, when he lost his eighteen-year-old son under tragic circumstances.

In the face of circumstances that would have caused many in his position to lose focus, he managed to hold himself together. The following season, his team won the Super Bowl. During all of the challenges, he continued to promote a vision of success for his team that fostered the commitment necessary to succeed at the highest level.

> *The first step toward creating an improved future is developing the ability to envision it. Vision will ignite the fire of passion that fuels our commitment to do whatever it takes to achieve excellence. Only vision allows us to transform dreams of greatness into the reality of achievement through human action. Vision has no boundaries and knows no limits. Our vision is what we become in life.*[5]—Tony Dungy

Building commitment is a necessity for effective leadership in all contexts.

This vision is often a primary source of inspiration that builds and sustains commitment. Partly, it is the belief that success *is* possible; it also focuses upon the reward and why it's important. However, it goes beyond even that. It requires forward thinking in that it must consider unknowns, acknowledge the fact that change is inevitable, and anticipate potential events in the future.

How Do Leaders Instill Vision?

When President Ronald Reagan stepped into office in his first term on January 20, 1981, America was at a low. The economy was suffering, inflation and interest rates were sky high, and a humiliating diplomatic crisis existed in Iran. Fifty-two American hostages had been held for 444 days. America had been disgraced, the public had lost much respect in leadership at the highest levels, and the Cold War with the Soviet Union was as imposing as ever. Confidence in the future of America had waned dramatically. National pride was almost nonexistent.

President Reagan was faced with an enormous challenge: how to bring positive and effective leadership back to a nation that had not experienced it, while in the midst of a weak economy and a foreign affairs debacle. One of the first steps he took was to begin instilling a positive "vision" for America. His vision was for America to regain pride in its accomplishments and look forward to a continuing legacy of freedom and prosperity, as established by its founders, to fulfill its special place in history. He spoke with passion and confidence about America as a "Shining City on a Hill."

> *The first step toward creating an improved future is developing the ability to envision it.*

However, President Reagan went far beyond words to promote a positive vision and restore America's reputation as a country that would not be humiliated by radical militants. Soon after taking office President Reagan put all enemies of America on notice that the U.S would not negotiate with anyone who might hold its citizens hostage. The new policy was that terrorism against the U.S. would meet with immediate reprisal.

Additionally President Reagan began implementing bold economic and fiscal policies that rewarded productivity and reduced taxes.[6] This began to foster economic recovery. Furthermore, during his administration, he convinced the Soviet Union that it could not win the Cold War, as he strengthened our military and pressed hard to stop the spread of communism. By the end of his second term, the Cold War was over. America had beaten the Soviet Union and was the world's only super power. His actions spoke louder than his words in realizing the positive vision he represented to America.

Vision is the blueprint of one's ultimate success. Effective leaders instill that sense of vision in others by stating the vision, describing how it can be attained, and then acting on it in a manner that will demonstrate the result. President Reagan's style of leadership was based upon building a vision that his constituents could support. He expressed his vision as founded upon his faith in God as well as the American dream. He communicated trust in the power of the free market to stimulate the economy. He expressed trust in the ability of American leaders to regain respect on the world stage. And he continually expressed his trust in the special potential of individuals to lead productive and meaningful lives without government assistance. The realization of his vision rekindled the American spirit and led to an economic and cultural turnaround unprecedented in American history.

Can a Leader Achieve Far Reaching Effects without Formal Authority or Power?

The accomplishments of great leaders are not about power. They are about results. And those results *must have benefit to others* or the leader cannot be characterized as a "great leader." One of the most moving leadership stories of the twentieth century had to do with a most unlikely person who went on to achieve a historical leadership role. She had practically no formal authority or power. But her influence led a revolution of human rights that is unsurpassed.

When Helen Keller was nineteen months old, she lost her hearing and sight due to a rare disease. As a result, she could not learn to speak. Like an animal, she could only utter guttural sounds to express her emotions and needs. For the next six years, she lost contact with others except through touch and smell. Her parents almost gave up hope that she would ever be able to lead a worthwhile life. But during this seemingly hopeless situation, her father, Arthur H. Keller, a former captain in the Confederate Army, pursued any and all options that might benefit his little daughter.

Captain Keller eventually was referred to a gifted special education teacher by the name of Anne Sullivan, who ultimately affected a life-changing miracle with the child. One bright May morning in 1888, behind the Keller home at the outdoor water pump, Sullivan's efforts to teach Helen words by spelling them into her hand finally paid off, even though she had no success in hundreds of previous attempts. Anne was pumping cool water on the child's hand and spelling "w-a-t-e-r" over and over to her.[7] Suddenly, in a dramatic moment, the little girl's awareness was awakened. She grasped the concept that every object has a name, and she could communicate with others if she learned to spell that name with her fingers. The same day, Helen learned many words before retiring, exhausted, to sleep that night.

In subsequent years, Helen became a prolific learner, and it was soon apparent

> *The accomplishments of great leaders are not about power. They are about results.*

that her willpower and persistence were far superior to other children. Despite her disability, Helen Keller became the most famous leader to champion the cause of the blind and deaf. She was an icon whose impact continues today. Because of her unusual ability to influence others, she inspired changes in public attitudes about the capabilities of people with disabilities.

Helen Keller pushed in an unrelenting manner for revolutionary changes in laws affecting people with disabilities. She garnered enormous influence with leaders in her time to benefit people with disabilities. Her influence and effective leadership opened countless doors of opportunity for access into mainstream education and employment. Ultimately, Helen Keller went on to inspire generations of people with disabilities to live worthwhile and fruitful lives. She unquestionably achieved great leadership status and benefited millions, despite having no formal authority and severe disabilities.

Is There a Best Style of Leadership?

Traditional debates about building effective leadership raise the question as to whether there is a best way to lead others. Is it authoritarian or collaborative; consensus based or charismatic based; enabling focused or some other style? In fact, the style or manner in which effective leaders engage with others and exercise their role is more a function of how they *respond* to the specific situation they face, rather than their own unique personality or abilities.

A leader faced with a split-second decision in a crisis that can lead to dire consequences may have to apply a highly directive style to avert a disaster. That same leader, in a different context, such as facilitating a strategy session or analyzing options for an organization's direction, may adopt a deferential and collaborative style to encourage input from staff members on how to solve problems creatively. It's the same leader in both instances, employing two very different styles to be successful.

Adopting the most effective leadership style to best fit the situation is an absolute necessity when leading others. Effective leaders must be flexible and adaptive to the unique requirements of the moment or the broad circumstances they face. In some cases, a forceful and quick acting style may be most appropriate; in other cases, a deliberate and patient style is necessary.

> *Adopting the most effective leadership style to best fit the situation is an absolute necessity when leading others.*

One of the twentieth century's most prominent leaders, Mahatma Gandhi (1869-1948), is considered the father of the Indian independence movement.[8] His leadership style was usually not forceful at all; in fact, it was calm, convincing, and deliberate, but enormously effective. By appealing to something his followers felt strongly about, independence from colonial rule, he *induced*, not forced, over two hundred million people in India to commit to the cause of winning independence. And while his leadership role and style required enormous courage, it did not require force to affect success.

Prior to his historic impact on India, Gandhi spent twenty years in South Africa, working to fight discrimination there. In the face of great opposition and threats, he worked to overcome discrimination by developing the concept of *Satyagraha*, a highly effective nonviolent way of fighting injustices through organized protests. "*Satyagraha*" means "insistence on truth." It can also be translated as "grasping onto principles" or the "truth force." Gandhi used that same style of leadership a second time when he worked successfully to remove British colonial rule in India.

Numerous civil rights leaders, including Martin Luther King Jr., used Gandhi's nonviolent protest style as a model to organize their followers in their own struggles. And they often had to demonstrate unrelenting courage in the face of personal risk. In 1959, with assistance of the American Friends Service Committee as well as the Quaker Group, King visited Gandhi's birthplace. There he was profoundly influenced by Gandhi's nonviolent activism and adopted such methods for use in the civil rights movement in the United States.

In a radio address made during his final evening in India,[9] King said:

> *Since being in India, I am more convinced than ever before that the method of nonviolent resistance is the most potent weapon available to oppressed people in their struggle for justice and human dignity. In a real sense, Mahatma Gandhi embodied in his life certain universal principles that are inherent in the moral structure of the universe, and these principles are as inescapable as the law of gravitation.*

King learned how to use nonviolent means to effect change, and he also learned about the critical role the leader's cause plays in establishing respect and commitment from others. The peaceful nonviolent leadership styles of both Gandhi and King demonstrate that it is possible to affect great historical shifts in governance as well as societal evolution without force.

Both cases, similar to Washington's case in war and Mother Teresa's case in missionary work, demonstrate the importance of a leader having to build commitment and the willingness of others to follow. And as demonstrated by President Reagan, the vision of positive outcomes must be communicated to followers to provide a rallying point for them to remain committed to the cause. Establishing such a commitment has to do not only with communicating and representing something followers can believe in, but building mutual respect between the leader and followers and forming a united foundation for a common cause and interests.

How Does a Leader Build Mutual Respect?

As referenced earlier, a leader must build deep and genuine respect in order to gain the commitment required to promote outstanding efforts from their followers. Formal authority, title, or words do not establish long-term and genuine respect. Respect is more a function of faith in and appreciation of what we do and represent than what we say.

General Robert E. Lee, who commanded the confederate forces during the Civil War, is still considered one of the most brilliant generals in history (despite surrendering to US forces in April 1865). For some, such respect seems a paradox, as the Civil War was primarily fought to maintain the iniquitous condition of slavery. But in fact, Lee actually opposed slavery and referred to it as a moral evil. Earlier in his life upon inheriting slaves from his deceased father-in-law, Lee immediately freed them. Speaking about the final outcome of the Civil War to Reverend John Leyburn in April 1869, Lee stated:

> *I am rejoiced that slavery is abolished. I believe it will be greatly for the interests of the South . . . . I would cheerfully*

have lost all I have lost by the war, and have suffered all I have suffered, to have this objective attained.[10]

General Lee opposed slavery and the secession of the South from the United States. But even more, he opposed the idea of the US government forcing the southern states to remain in the Union under what many considered to be disparaging and oppressive governance. He believed that individual states should have the right to govern their affairs without interference of the federal government. Furthermore, he held the position that states should have the right to enact their own laws as well as direct trade, establish public policy, and manage their internal affairs of governance on their own.

Reluctantly, Lee resigned his federal commission in the US Army and was subsequently appointed commander of confederate forces. Remarkably, even though he led an army in a highly controversial context, and ultimately suffered defeat, at the end of the war he was not tried as a traitor; in fact, he was held in high esteem by all, including most of his former foes. How is it that General Lee garnered so much respect from his troops, from his foes, and subsequently from historians?

> *Genuine respect is more a function of faith in and appreciation of what we do and represent than what we say.*

Perhaps one of the most telling compliments about Lee that explains why he was so highly respected was paid by Booker T. Washington:

> *The first white people in America, certainly the first in the South, to exhibit their interest in the reaching of the Negro and saving his soul through the medium of the Sunday-school, were Robert E. Lee and Stonewall Jackson.*[11]

Even Lee's primary opponent, Ulysses S. Grant, the commander of the Union Army, respected General Lee so much that upon cessation of hostilities, he petitioned President Lincoln to allow Lee to return to personal life without trial as a traitor.

General Lee's actions demonstrated unusually high principles, which illustrated to others that he was genuinely concerned for the well-being of all people, even his enemy. As an example, he demanded that all captives be treated humanely. His Christian faith, the cornerstone of his character, and his desire to live the Golden Rule were demonstratively paramount in his life.[12]

For leaders to build such mutual respect between themselves and others, they must first demonstrate respect by treating others with respect, even those with whom they disagree. People do not long respect anyone who does not demonstrate respect for them. In the case of the leadership role, this fact is even truer.

Establishing mutual respect begins with the leader. Leaders must demonstrate real interest in caring for those they lead and treat them with dignity as well as showing concern for their welfare. This ability is an undeniable measure of one's character. The character of a leader cannot be hidden for long. In time it will be revealed, and when it is, those within the sphere of the leader's authority will respond with respect or disrespect.

How Does a Leader Demonstrate Character?

Dwight D. Eisenhower was the supreme commander of the Allied Forces in Europe during World War II. He then went on to become the thirty-fourth president of the United States from 1953 until 1961. His two terms were arguably the most peaceful and prosperous in American history.

> *The supreme quality for leadership is unquestionably integrity. Without it, no real success is possible.*—Dwight D. Eisenhower

Integrity is the opposite of hypocrisy. It refers to the habit of demonstrating consistency between words and actions. It places truthfulness and accuracy in genuine communications as a top priority. A person with integrity demonstrates values, principles, and outcomes that are consistent with their words. This level of internal consistency establishes integrity as a virtue that is definitive of the core of a person's being.

In his "I Have a Dream" speech, Martin Luther King proposed that the ultimate measure of the worth of a person should focus on the level of their character. In his view, this should be placed higher than any other attribute. Dispelling the practice of considering a person's ethnic origination in assessing them, he maintained that a person's true worth is established by what they are, as opposed to what they say or from where they originate. He discounted material wealth and social status as valid measures of a person's value.

Leaders are by the nature of their role held to a higher standard for modeling character. And because leaders at all levels are entrusted with the responsibility and authority to guide others toward success, their character is critical to their long-term success and legacy. Integrity is the keystone in the foundation of their character.

Abraham Lincoln epitomized leadership founded upon character. He demonstrated to the public that our character is much more than just what we display for others to see; it is what genuinely lies deep within the self. As a result, Lincoln became an icon of great leadership in American history, largely due to his demonstration of character through his actions.

> *Reputation is the shadow. Character is the tree.*—Abraham Lincoln

James Lindgren, of the International World History Project, in his "Ranking Our Presidents" (a survey project jointly sponsored by the *Wall Street Journal* and the Federalist Society), assessed forty-two presidents from Washington through Clinton. Lincoln ranked first, in large part due to the admiration his character and principles garnered from all who responded to the survey. James Taranto and Leonard Leo conducted a study in 2004 in which they

Leaders are by the nature of their role held to a higher standard for modeling character.

ranked US presidents from the best to worst.[13] They found that scholars in the fields of politics as well as history ranked Lincoln as the number one choice. And of all ranking polls conducted since 1948, Lincoln has been rated at the top each time.

In *What Color is a Conservative? My Life and Politics,* former Congressman J. C. Watts of Oklahoma emphasizes the non-self-promotional nature of true character as being at the heart of all great leadership. Watts makes the case that a person's character is founded upon selflessness and the level of integrity they demonstrate as well as promote.

> *Integrity is doing the right thing when no one is watching.*—C.S. Lewis

But whether anyone is watching closely or not, a leader's true character (or lack of character) will eventually be revealed in time.

Nicknamed the "Iron Lady," Margaret Thatcher served as the prime minister of Great Britain from 1979 through 1990. The only woman to have ever held the office, she was known for her unusually high standards of character. She not only championed the importance of moral character in her public addresses, she established the platform of well founded character in her leadership style. Her reputation for demonstrating integrity was so impeccable that not even her critics could rationally question her political motives and passion for service to her country.

In September 1987, Thatcher defined her own political philosophy, one that embodied her character, saying:

> *I think we have gone through a period when too many children and people have been given to understand "I have a problem, it is the government's job to cope with it," or "I have a problem, I will go and get a grant to cope with it," or "I am homeless, the government must house me," and so they are casting their problems on society, and who is society? There is no such thing! There are individual men and women and*

> there are families, and no government can do anything except through people, and people look to themselves first. It is our duty to look after ourselves and then also to help look after our neighbor. Life is a reciprocal business, and people have got the entitlements too much in mind without the obligations.[14]

Thatcher's statement applies as much today as it did in 1987 or at any time in history. She further asserted:

> If you do not provide, you cannot be certain that anyone else will. Living beyond your means leads to dependency instead of independence, and dependency leads to degradation. This is as true for nations as it is for individuals.

The "degradation" of which she spoke is the logical outcome of the lack of character. In essence, the Iron Lady believed that it is the responsibility of citizens to demonstrate self-reliance and not to routinely expect the state or others to take care of them. However, she did assert that when necessary, it is the duty of those who can to assist others in need. This spirit of selflessness and service to others was at the center of her life in her private and public service. Her sterling integrity made for one of the best illustrations of how solid character is at the heart of all great leaders.

Where Do Knowledge and Decision Skills Enter the Leadership Equation?

Each of the leaders referenced so far, from General Washington through Margaret Thatcher, demonstrated character. Their principles, vision, and ability to build commitment and inspire others enabled them to garner power and influence. However, that was not enough to make them successful. Throughout history, some leaders have obtained power and influence only to lead their countries, organizations, or followers to disastrous ends because of poor decisions.

Regardless of other outstanding attributes, leaders are not likely to be successful without possessing the knowledge and decision skills that enable them to navigate through countless potential pitfalls in order to find the right path. The knowledge of the leaders we are examining was in large part a function of their experience and intellect. However, none of the leaders we have referenced knew everything. And each, realizing that, allowed others to provide input, perspective, expertise, and critical knowledge necessary to result in success.

At times, almost all leaders must take charge and be assertive, possibly even authoritarian if it will save lives. When US Airways Flight 1549 hit a flock of geese and both engines quit in January 2009, there was no time for Captain Chesley Sullenberger to deliberate on options or collaborate with superiors. The captain had only a moment to decide what to do. If he had tried to deliberate more or follow the recommendations of the control tower (which had told him to try to return to the runway), it is unlikely there would have been survivors. But when there is time, leaders do have to step back and be collaborative, be willing to allow others to challenge and disagree with them in weighing options to help make better decisions and develop effective strategy.

> *Regardless of other outstanding attributes, leaders are not likely to be successful without possessing strong decision skills.*

Similar to the practical knowledge that applies to leadership roles, effective decision skills are not something most people will learn in academic or theoretical contexts. They are best learned through real life experience, often through failure. It is believed by many historians that General Washington actually held leadership positions in more battles lost than won. However, he learned from those losses and failures. And as a direct result, he became a better leader and tactician.

Washington, Thatcher, and the others all learned through practical experience that effective decision skills require integrating multiple functions. Patience, fact finding, astute analysis, and informed intuition are each necessary to enable a leader, at any level, to make effective decisions. In many critical cases, a successful leader has to consider lessons from the past, assess the requirements of the present, and look forward to future possibilities in the process before deciding.

Decision making at its most basic level is an exercise in independence. Effective leaders do not place undue emphasis upon the popularity of their actions or decisions. If leaders fret about what others may say about their actions, they are deferring to considerations that likely obviate principle as well as the often difficult course that is required for real and lasting success. They must be able to think on their own. And this requires a measure of independence and confidence unfettered by fearing lack of approval or undue concern over political considerations.

Outstanding leaders who exercise independent thought are not often satisfied with the status quo. They are often effective change agents. Though they may work well in team contexts and share in decisions, their ability to think independently and creatively usually makes them strong individualists. That is one of the primary reasons they rise to leadership positions. Individual thought is a prerequisite to effective decision skills and problem solving. This will be even more so in the Twenty-First Century.

Why Are Leadership Skills so Requisite for Success in the Twenty-First Century?

While much of today's way of life is dominated by technology, there remains an unalterable fact in regards to human dynamics. Someone or some group in a leadership position will always be making decisions and exercising power to influence and affect others. Whether serving at the highest levels of government, business, educational institutions, public service, or any arena where people must work together for a common goal, there will be a leader.

A teacher in a classroom, a soccer coach, the head of a volunteer group, a student organizing a social event, or the head of a family is each in a leadership position. As addressed earlier, even persons without formal authority, who have the opportunity to influence and suggest options or new ideas to others, play some level of a leadership role. This inescapable fact is now heightened as a result of instantaneous sharing of information through technology as well as online social contact. This makes leadership skills more important for anyone to have value in organizations or attain success in most endeavors.

What Is Principle-Based Leadership?

Principle-based leadership is leading based upon a foundation of values that ultimately promotes success and results that benefit others. Principle-based leaders assume positions of authority fundamentally because they are responsible individuals. They are honest and genuinely desire to benefit others and make constructive contributions beyond their own self-interest. The principles they embody, which are grounded in character with integrity at the center, represent the noblest nature of the human spirit.

Principle-based leadership is not a style; it is a function of one's values regardless of the specific leadership style adopted. It is what the leader is *about*. Whether using a direct and authoritative style or a collaborative and deliberate style, principle-based leadership, in its most elemental form, is demonstrated by a set of core values that define the character of the leader. It does not necessarily include an absolute set of principles or values, but it does include standards that universally demonstrate an admirable character, build mutual respect and trust, and attain commitment from others.

When Washington assumed command of the Continental army during the American Revolution, and then later when he became the nation's first president, he accepted those roles not because he wanted power, but because others appealed to his basic desire to serve. They recognized that his talents, intelligence, and character were unmatched among his peers; they pressed him into leading the Continental army and becoming president even though he did not initially aspire to either.

Washington did not long for power. But he did long to see his country freed from the tyranny being imposed by Great Britain, and that is why he accepted the command of the Continental army. Later he recognized that for the new nation to survive, it would require a leader who could unite the thirteen independent states under a common direction or the Union would soon expire. Because of his love for his country above his personal convenience, Washington agreed to lead.

Mother Teresa was a Catholic nun who never aspired to wield the enormous influence she eventually had on a worldwide scale. She simply pursued a path of service that eventually had a positive impact upon millions. She accepted the great responsibility and challenge of a worldwide ministry because of the principles that guided her life.

> *Principle-based leadership is leading based upon a foundation of values that ultimately promote success and results that benefit others.*

Martin Luther King began his life of service as a Baptist minister with the simple desire to bring others to Christ. He did not begin with a plan to one day become a historical figure. Yet ultimately, because of his core principles, he assumed a leadership position. He accepted all of the risks and challenges in a spirit of service that ultimately led to his martyrdom but benefited millions.

Ronald Reagan, when questioned about what spurred him to his historical role in America prevailing in the Cold War against the Soviet Union, cited one central principle. It was his unrelenting will and commitment to not compromise his efforts to stop communism. For example, though his advisors cautioned him against strong and challenging language when speaking at the Berlin Wall, in June 1987, he challenged USSR's leader, Mikhail Gorbachev, with his "tear down this wall!" statement. It was representative of his unwillingness to compromise principles for politics.[15]

Reagan's advisors had suggested he tone down his speech and avoid any direct challenges to the Soviet Union.[16] But Reagan continued to maintain, in unrelenting and dramatic terms, that the Berlin Wall was representative of the kind of repression that was counter to the basic human need for freedom on all levels:

> *Behind me stands a wall that encircles the free sectors of this city, part of a vast system of barriers that divides the entire continent of Europe . . . . Standing before the Brandenburg Gate, every man is a German, separated from his fellow men. Every man is a Berliner, forced to look upon a scar . . . . As long as this gate is closed, as long as this scar of a wall is permitted to stand, it is not the German question alone that remains open, but the question of freedom for all mankind . . . . General Secretary Gorbachev, if you seek peace, if you seek prosperity for the Soviet Union and Eastern Europe, if you seek liberalization, come here to this gate. Mr. Gorbachev, open this gate! Mr. Gorbachev, tear down this wall!*

Each of the highly effective and revered leaders described so far are united by at least one common denominator. It is that they were *principled* leaders whose integrity and character were at the core of their being. They were trusted to be open and honest about their goals; steadfast in the face of personal risk; humble even after great success; truthful; models of moral character; and committed to putting the interests of others before themselves in the spirit of service. That is the formula defined by principle-based leadership. As has been the case throughout history, the most positive progress during the twenty-first century will likely be attributed most to those whose principles are at the core of how they lead.

Chapter 1 Summary

- *Leadership* is service to others, and it is best demonstrated not by words but by action.
- *Building commitment* is a core necessity for effective leadership in every context in which a leader must direct the efforts of others.
- There is no universal "*best*" style of leadership, only knowing what style is best for the specific circumstance and then applying that style as appropriate.
- Effective leadership is the ability to set and promote *positive direction* for others and gain their commitment to follow.
- Principle-based leadership is demonstrated by a set of *core values* that define the character of the leader.
- *Integrity* is the most fundamental building block of principle-based leadership.
- *Mutual respect* is a requisite for all successful leadership roles.

CHAPTER 2
UNIVERSAL LEADERSHIP QUALITIES

In 1960, during the first televised presidential campaign debate between John F. Kennedy and Richard M. Nixon, an interesting result occurred. Radio audiences who only listened to that debate without the benefit of watching were polled, and the results favored Nixon.[17] And many commentators and political pundits indicated that Nixon's responses demonstrated a much firmer grasp of the issues, and his greater experience in foreign affairs was obvious.

However, the polls of television audiences indicated a different result. They had seen how Nixon, in a light grey suit, blended into the wall behind him. The heat of the camera light placed directly above his head caused sweat to form on his brow. His unshaven face combined with the pallor from a recent illness made Nixon appear disheveled and even a little apprehensive as his eyes shifted rapidly from side to side.

Kennedy had worn a charcoal suit that made him stand out on the black-and-white television screen. The camera lights were not directly over his head, and he appeared relaxed and comfortable as he spoke directly and confidently into the camera. When television audiences were surveyed, the handsome and charismatic Kennedy was favored by a significant margin. The audience was far less attuned to the spoken content of his actual words than to his impressive appearance and the presidential image he conveyed.

As illustrated during the debate, image is critical in determining outward impressions of leaders. And outward images are often all voters or constituents have to go on when they do not have direct contact with leaders. This is particularly true when observing leaders from afar, such as heads of state, government officials, corporate heads, or popular media figures. But when leaders work alongside or closely with others, image is often proven far less important than practical skills such as decisiveness, competence, listening, or demonstrating how to work in the best interests of others.

From the middle of the twentieth century to the present, countless studies and research projects have been conducted by universities, the military, corporations, and public sector organizations to identify important universal leadership qualities.[18] In such attempts to define leadership, the skills and qualities those studies identified as most important were dependent upon the *specific context* of the leadership roles being examined.[19] Studies that focused upon contexts in which leaders had direct contact with followers almost all highlight the importance of qualities such as building genuine rapport and mutual respect, task focus and competence, and participative leadership.[20]

Leadership Contexts

Obviously direct contact contexts are by far where most people observe firsthand how leadership skills are practiced. These contexts are those in which the leader has regular interaction directly with those they lead. Effective leadership in such contexts will invariably be enhanced by good interactive skills and the ability to promote results. However, regardless of the context, there is always one quality absolutely essential for leading. That quality is *influence*. If a person has no significant influence with others, regardless of their position or title, that person is unable to lead.

As referenced in chapter 1, leadership requires knowledge, skills, and abilities that vary depending upon the situation and other variables of the role and circumstances. However, as with the basic fact that principled leaders are generally more respected, there are also universal leadership qualities that generally yield more positive results regardless of the context or role the leader fulfils.

In surveys of hundreds of adults and students in leadership roles over a twenty-five year period using the Most Preferred Leader Questionnaire (MPLQ; see Appendix I), there is a fairly consistent set of leadership qualities and behaviors that stand out regardless of the age of the respondent or the specific context. The leaders chosen by respondents in the MPLQ as having the most positive influence typically included supervisors at work, managers, coaches, teachers, parents or family members, and other persons who had regular direct contact with the respondent.

> *Direct contact contexts are by far where most people observe firsthand how leadership skills are practiced.*

In the MPLQ's open-ended format, the most frequent descriptions defined leaders or mentors who listen well, care much about the interests of others, were helpful and encouraging, and demonstrated admirable qualities such as integrity and selflessness. Other characteristics, including fostering good decisions and the ability to handle risk, were often listed. Qualities such as image or oratory skills were rarely mentioned.

The results of the MPLQ cited here only include responses from those that had served in leadership positions or gained recognition as high achievers. The role of the person identified most often by the participants in the survey as having the greatest positive influence was someone *in their direct family.* Over a third of the respondents cited a parent or family member. This result underscores the importance that good parenting can play in the development of leaders and high achievers.

Universal Leadership Qualities

Based upon compilations of results from administering the MPLQ to individuals and groups and subsequent discussions of results with them, twelve leadership qualities especially relevant in direct contact contexts have been defined:

- Confidence
- Courage
- Decisiveness
- Encouragement
- Excellence
- Foresight
- Influence
- Integrity
- Listening
- Mutual trust
- Self-discipline
- Service focused

Charting the Responses

The open-ended responses have been categorized within one of the above twelve dimensions. However, the exact terms respondents used may not have been exactly the same wording as the twelve dimensions. For example, anything having to do with "caring" is included under encouragement or "honesty" under integrity. The "all other" category includes additional dimensions such as image, persuasiveness or building alliances (political skills). However, such items were reported so infrequently that they are placed under the "all other" category. While reviewing and comparing the scores of the dimensions on the chart consider that even the lower scoring dimensions are very essential. For example, service focused was more important by itself than everything included together in the "all other" category. The full description of each of the twelve categories as interpreted from the open-ended responses is provided below the chart.

Percentage Responses to the MPLQ Survey

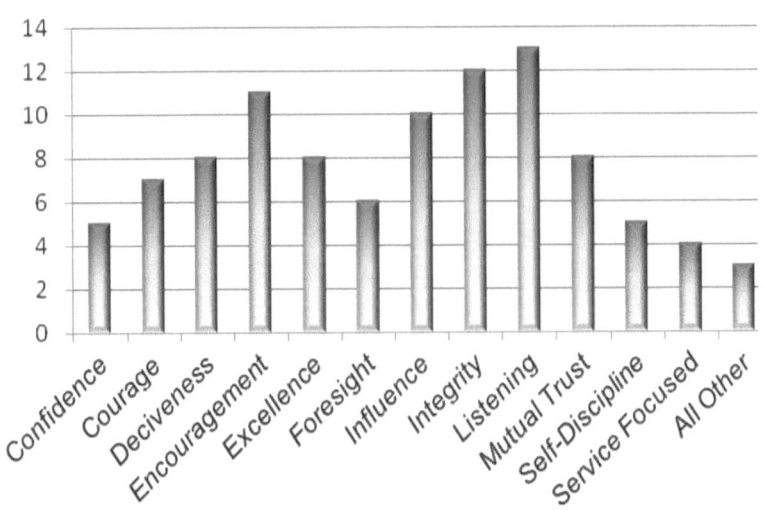

Confidence

Leaders who demonstrate well-founded confidence are much more likely to exercise significant positive influence in direct contact contexts. It's important to emphasize there is a difference between confidence in *purpose* versus confidence in *abilities*. Obviously, both are important, but one has to do with the validity and value of one's direction, while the other has to do with one's ability to affect results.

Well-founded confidence is emphasized, because if it is not grounded in fact or reality, it's not likely it will evoke genuine credibility or respect. There is an important difference between confidence and arrogance. Overconfidence, which often manifests itself in arrogant behavior, isn't grounded in fact and is likely to have more to do with ego or self-promotion. It is inclined to evoke misdirection, poor decisions, and even resentment from others. Arrogant behavior may sometimes be a ruse to cover up a lack of self-confidence or even insecurity.

Genuine and well-founded self-confidence is often attended by humility. Boasting or bragging is not part of it. When questioned about his achievements, whether in foreign or domestic affairs, President Reagan almost always discounted his personal abilities. The humility he displayed in questions about himself was consistent during his service as the governor of California and as president. Reagan's confidence was not so much in his own abilities, but rather the *causes or principles* he represented. In his farewell address to the nation on January 11, 1989, he stated, "I wasn't a great communicator, but I communicated great things, and they didn't spring full bloom from my brow, they came from the heart of a great nation."

The ability to remain confident under stress or criticism is an absolutely essential quality of effective leaders. That is not to say good leaders are oblivious to others counsel or advice but are in fact open to it while still not losing sight of their ability to affect important goals and results. As so well expressed in the words of Rudyard Kipling in his poem 'If', such persons remain confident in the face of criticism.

> *If you can keep your head when all about you are losing theirs*
> *and blaming it on you; if you can trust yourself when all men*
> *doubt you, yet make allowance for their doubting too . . .*

Courage

There is some measure of risk inherent in almost all leadership contexts. This is particularly true when it has to do with an important cause or commitment of resources. But there is also risk inherent in practically any context where a decision is necessary. One choice may result in gain and the other in loss (sometimes significant loss). The ability to handle risk rationally and with composure is at the core of most important leadership roles. Effective leaders, while alert to potential loss, do not allow themselves to be intimidated by the fear of failure or making a mistake. In fact, that is one of the most consistent characteristics of strong leaders: they are willing to shoulder risk. And they are willing to take responsibility when things under their authority go wrong.

It is important to emphasize that good leaders discern between risk that is worth taking and risk that is not worth taking. However, sometimes there is no choice, and the leader must have the courage to act in a decisive manner in the face of unavoidable risk. Courage is not the lack of fear; it is the ability to overcome fear and take necessary action.

Captain Chesley Sullenberger, pilot of the ill-fated Flight 1549, was interviewed about the event on the *60 Minutes*. During the interview, he stated that the moments before the crash were the most fearful he had ever experienced in his life. He had no hesitation in explaining that the emotion of fear was a very significant part of his challenge to handle during the crisis.

But undaunted by fear or overcome by emotion, Sullenberger

> *Genuine and well-founded self-confidence is often attended by humility.*

maintained his composure and made the unorthodox yet correct decision to set the plane down in the freezing waters of the Hudson River, saving the lives of all 155 persons aboard. Even after the plane was in the icy waters, Sullenberger toured the unflooded part of the passenger cabin twice to make sure everyone had evacuated before being the last to leave the aircraft.

Decisiveness

Decisiveness is a requisite for effective leadership. This is not just the willingness to make difficult decisions, but the patience and intelligence to make the best decision practical within the scope of the leader's responsibility.

Making good decisions is often challenging for at least two reasons. The first is the necessity of having to gather the most relevant information in a timely manner, consider all the options, and assess the likely consequences of each option. The second is that deciding to do the *right* thing is usually more difficult than doing the convenient or politically expedient thing. It takes character to make good decisions, especially in leadership positions.

> *When one bases his life on principle, 99 percent of his decisions are already made.*—Author unknown

As demonstrated by Captain Sullenberger, quick decisions are often necessary in a crisis. Had the captain spent too much time deliberating, it is likely that many lives would have been lost. L. G. Elliott, the Canadian-born prize-winning physicist, cautioned against indecision:

> *Vacillating people seldom succeed. Successful men and women are very careful in reaching their decisions, and very persistent and determined in action thereafter.*

Effective decision makers do not always make quick decisions, but timeliness combined with due diligence is a formula for more effective decisions.

Encouragement

> *Too often we underestimate the power of a touch, a smile, a kind word, a listening ear, an honest compliment, or the smallest act of caring, all of which have the power to turn a life around.*—Leo Buscaglia

Encouragement is the most essential activity that lifts and supports

> **Decisiveness is a requisite for effective leadership.**

the efforts of others. It often has an enormously positive effect upon a person's self-image and self-worth. Examples of activities that enable leaders to encourage others within their span of influence include validating them, demonstrating confidence in their abilities, and demonstrating genuine interest in their successes.

Our chief want is someone who will inspire us to be what we know we could be.—Ralph Waldo Emerson

Encouragement of others, whether through words or actions, is an absolute necessity in all leadership contexts.

Our words can uplift and heal and empower—or not. Words can inspire, rekindle a sense of wonder, and provide direction, or they can dampen spirits, condemn ideas, and destroy initiative. We've all seen examples of this. Words can be used to delight and provide comfort . . . . Words can bring peace to a family, they can restore a soul, they can certainly instruct and provide counsel, and they can encourage the downtrodden, strengthen the weak, and lift those who have fallen.—Tony Dungy

Excellence

The most effective leaders are ones who set standards to which others aspire. They model behavior that is admirable and worthy of attainment. They demonstrate excellence in most endeavors in which they participate, whether that is how they perform their duties, how they conduct their personal affairs, their own level of health and fitness, or how they treat others.

Leaders who are guided by high principles generally demonstrate excellence at most activities because excellence is a habit that affects the entire person.

Excellence is an art won by training and habituation. We do not act rightly because we have virtue or excellence, but rather have those because we have acted rightly. We are what we repeatedly do. Excellence then is not an act but a habit.—Aristotle

The most successful leaders in all fields, from business to sports, are persons who not only demonstrate excellence, they encourage and teach it. This is especially true when such leaders are in close contact with others.

> *The quality of a person's life is in direct proportion to their commitment to excellence, regardless of their chosen field or endeavor.*—Vince Lombardi

Foresight

Foresight in leadership contexts is the ability to anticipate challenges and opportunities before they become obvious. It is forward thinking with a focus beyond the present. In some respects, it is creative, as the

> *The most effective leaders are ones who set standards to which others aspire.*

leader must think outside existing circumstances and parameters to identify new or unique ways to solve problems or identify new paths toward success. Foresight is preparing for the future.

While always mindful of what has worked in the past, leaders with astute foresight are unbounded by convention or traditional ways of doing things. Such leaders are often initiators of change, but only when appropriate. For leaders with a keen sense of foresight, change is not an end in itself, as that rarely guarantees success. But necessary change is a process applied only when judicious, and then it is guided by prudence, after carefully considering options and potential outcomes. Foresight may be defined as the "ability to connect the dots," because it integrates and connects seemingly unrelated considerations to determine the best course for the future.

In 1975, Alan Hald, a young Arizona entrepreneur with an eye on the future, met the editor of a new magazine for computer hobbyists at a convention in Los Angeles. Talking with the editor, Hald became aware of potential trends in technology that would eventually make it possible for anyone to own a computer. At the time, only governments and big businesses could afford computers.

Stimulated by his new awareness of technology trends, Hald had the foresight to see that the future of computers would be very different from the past, and many new business opportunities could open up. After the convention, Hald went home with the idea of starting a hobby computer store. As cofounder of MicroAge Inc., Hald ultimately guided the company's growth from only one location in 1976 to a $6 billion Fortune 500 company with over a thousand franchises worldwide. Hald's foresight enabled him to develop a business that employed thousands and contributed immeasurably to the proliferation of the personal computer industry.

Influence

> *Leadership is influence . . . . People buy into the leader before they buy into the vision.* —John C. Maxwell

At the core of leading is the ability to influence others. Whether between two people or on an unlimited scale, the leader is the determining factor in the direction or action adopted. Leading in direct contact contexts is a distinctly personal dynamic, affecting the efforts as well as the desires and the motives of others. Outstanding leaders, especially those who bring out the best in others, appeal not only to the rational and objective but often more to the emotional and personal side of those they influence. This

> *While always mindful of what has worked in the past, leaders with astute foresight are unbounded by convention or traditional ways of doing things.*

is what enabled Washington and Gandhi to lead their followers to success in the causes they represented, even in the face of physical harm or loss of life.

On May 13, 1940, Winston Churchill delivered his first speech as prime minister in the House of Commons in Great Britain. His nation was being attacked by the mighty German Luftwaffe, which along with German storm troopers had been rolling unabated across Eastern Europe. The British people were terrorized by the looming threat of annihilation by their foe. Churchill's words in that first speech were perhaps as influential as any words spoken in human history. They ultimately galvanized and then focused the will and spirit of his countrymen to overcome fear and to fight against overwhelming odds when things appeared all but lost:

> *I would say to the House as I said to those who have joined this government: I have nothing to offer but blood, toil, tears, and sweat. We have before us an ordeal of the most grievous kind. We have before us many, many long months of struggle and of suffering . . . . You ask what is our policy? I will say it is to wage war with all our might, with all the strength that God can give us, to wage war against a monstrous tyranny never surpassed in the dark, lamentable catalogue of human crime. You ask what is our aim? I can answer in one word: Victory. Victory at all costs. Victory in spite of all terror. Victory however long and hard the road may be. For without victory there is no survival.*

Churchill's words and unrelenting defiance of the Nazi war machine served as a rallying cry in Great Britain's struggle against Germany in those dark times. And ultimately Great Britain along with the Allied Forces would defeat Nazi Germany by May of 1945.

Integrity

Integrity, while driven by values, is best illustrated by actions. It is demonstrated by what a leader does and encourages in his or her span of influence. Hector Ruiz, CEO of Advanced Nanotechnology Solutions, illustrated how integrity may be established as a cultural cornerstone of an organization at every level.

> *At the core of leading is the ability to influence others.*

Ruiz was born in Piedras Negras, Coahuila, Mexico, near the border of Texas. His family lived in poverty, and he had no financial means through his teenage years. After he learned to speak English, he attended high school in Eagle Pass, Texas, walking across the Mexico-Texas border. He graduated as the valedictorian of his class and then attended the University of Texas at Austin, earning a BS and an MS in electrical engineering. Ruiz then went on to Rice University, where he earned a PhD in 1973. Eventually he worked his way up to become the CEO of Advanced Nanotechnology Solutions.

Sought as a speaker and commentator on success and leadership, Ruiz was often asked about how he built his success. When interviewed in 2005 by *Fortune* magazine, he referred to the critical requirement for building and leading organizations with a foundation based on integrity:

> *Surround yourself with people of integrity, and get out of their way. In my adult years as a manager, Bob Galvin, the former CEO of Motorola, was my most influential leader. He told me, "A good leader knows he is doing a good job when he knows with certainty that he can say yes to anything his staff asks and feel totally confident that they will do the right thing." If you surround yourself with the right people who have integrity, and they all understand well the goals and objectives of the organization, then the best thing to do as a leader is to get out of their way. I use this advice quite a bit at work. The right people will feel far more pressure to performing well when they are trusted.*

Ruiz's emphasis upon integrity was essential to his style of leadership, which required complete trust in his team. Integrity ensures that your words and actions can be trusted as honest and forthright so others may be sure that you will do what you say you intend to. Without that level of trust, Ruiz would not have been able to step back

Integrity, while driven by values, is best illustrated by actions.

and allow his staff the level of leadership necessary to function with creativity and confidence.

Listening

Today more than ever, people are inundated with information overload and interruptions. Distractions such as cell phones, computers, iPods, and 24/7 news channels bombard us continuously. As a result, people have become more effective at screening out information than absorbing it. Even when listening, there is often the natural continual chattering in our brain, formulating an answer or reacting to what is being said even before the other party has finished speaking.

All people want to express something, but too few want to listen. Often they hear the words but do not hear the true content of the message. Additionally, their knowledge, beliefs, and opinions may lead to prejudgments, which stifle the humble activity of opening the mind to someone's message, needs, or values. A failure to learn the important skill of listening results in a closed mind.

Listening and being genuinely open to the perspectives of others is requisite to all effective human dynamics. For leaders, it is even more critical, because no one can truly lead people who don't believe they will be listened to. This is not to say that the leader must go along with a different perspective. It does mean the leader must demonstrate conscientious consideration of all rational and well-communicated positions, regardless of the source. Strong listening skills indicate openness and sincere engagement. They indicate regard for others, which is a primary requirement for promoting mutual respect as well as a foundation for influence.

> *Wisdom is the reward you get for a lifetime of listening when you'd have preferred to talk.*—Doug Larsen

Mutual Trust

Most respondents in the MPLQ surveys cited appreciation for trusting relationships with the leaders they found to be most influential. Genuine relationships between people are in part a function of regular open and honest communications.

> *It is mutual trust, even more than mutual interest, that holds human associations together.*—H. L. Mencken

Trust is a two-way street in which both parties must listen and share the truth about important issues and events. This is just as true in the work place as it is in the home. And this measure of trust is an absolute prerequisite for principle-based leaders to build sound relationships and the commitment necessary for positive influence. Trust is similar to mutual respect, in that it is practically impossible to build without reciprocation.

The kind of trust established by principle-based leaders is founded upon transparency, a much touted activity but one too infrequently practiced by those in high positions. In addition to genuine openness, transparency requires demonstrating trust in the reliability of others. This in fact has an important self-worth-building quality.

> *Few things help an individual more than to place responsibility upon him, and to let him know that you trust him.*—Booker T. Washington

Self-Discipline

Before, during and after his presidency, Harry S. Truman was a student of great leaders. He learned that leaders practiced self-discipline in order to affect great results.

> *In reading the lives of great men, I found that the first victory they won was over themselves . . . . Self-discipline with all of them came first.*

How can leaders develop true respect if they don't demonstrate self-discipline? They can't. This is especially true when they are in direct contact with those they lead. In most cultures, from the Spartans of ancient Greece to Japanese Samurai to the United States Marines during World War II and the Navy SEALs of today, self-discipline is the first step toward building leaders. In essence, it has first to do with mastery over the self: mentally, physically, and spiritually.

In their excellent handbook on developing practical leadership skills, *Leadership 2.0,* Bradberry and Greaves[21] provide an excellent blueprint of how leaders can strengthen self-mastery. They refer to the concept of "emotional intelligence" and its utility for leaders learning to exercise self-discipline. Bradberry and Greaves list four dimensions within the sphere of emotional intelligence which are essential for self-discipline:

1. Self-awareness: the ability to accurately perceive your emotions in the moment and understand your tendencies across situations. This enables leaders to more effectively make sense of their emotions and avoid being sidetracked by them. At the same time, they may harness emotional energy for constructive means.
2. Self-management: the ability to use awareness of one's emotions to stay flexible and better direct behavior toward positive outcomes. This means managing emotional reactions to people and situations. It is not so much suppressing emotions as not allowing them to overrule rational decisions and behavior. This is often displayed by the words leaders use. And the kind of language leaders use says a lot about their character (or lack thereof).
3. Social awareness: picking up on the emotions of other people and understanding what is influencing their behavior and needs. This requires an astute sense of tuning in to others, whether through listening, observing, or learning more about them through their actions.
4. Relationship management: This dimension is made better as a function of a firm grasp of the first three dimensions. It is built upon heightened awareness of the emotions of the leader and others. It integrates objective information from

all sides to manage interactions more successfully. It fosters improved communications and resolution to disagreements or conflict.

Lack of self-discipline can't be masked or hidden. It doesn't take long for most in close contact with a leader to determine if that leader has self-discipline. It will be revealed in their behavior and demeanor. It will be displayed in their attitude. And self-discipline can even be indicated by physical appearance. It is no accident that persons who are healthy and fit very often have an advantage in gaining the respect of others and influencing them. If those in a leadership position do not demonstrate self-respect, they will hindered significantly in gaining the respect of others.

While self-discipline may conjure up images of self-denial or an unpleasant lifestyle, the fact is that self-discipline is freedom, because it opens the door to more rewarding fulfillment than does mediocrity or hedonism. As noted by Stephen Covey, "The undisciplined are slaves to moods, appetites, and passions."[22] Lack of self-discipline may manifest itself in addictions or any of a number of forms. But most importantly, those without self-discipline lack will power and the strength necessary to live a fruitful life and to become a leader others will aspire to model.

Service Focused

Service focused leaders demonstrate that they are sincerely interested in the welfare and the activities of others. Such leadership may be demonstrated through the responsibility a leader assumes or through person-to-person interactions.

In all cases, there is *involvement* in the interest of others. This is a function of a leader's values. It is often a driver for the leader's direction as well as priorities. Leaders who care about others do not prove it by just saying they care. They prove it by their involvement, demonstrating both compassion and action. Tim Tebow, the two-time Heisman Trophy winner and one of the most successful college football quarterbacks of all time, emphasizes the importance of *serving others* in leadership roles:[23]

> Strong leaders encourage you to do things for your own benefit, not just theirs.

Mother Teresa's service in ministry for over forty-five years was modeled after Christ, her own personal servant leader. She didn't have to talk about it; she simply

> *It doesn't take long for most in close contact with a leader to determine if that leader has self-discipline.*

demonstrated her desire to serve in a caring manner through her actions:

> Being unwanted, unloved, uncared for, forgotten by everybody, I think that is a much greater hunger, a much greater poverty than the person who has nothing to eat.

Mother Teresa believed being unloved was such a great burden for so many that she continuously worked to make others feel that they were cared for through the *self-sacrificing leadership service* of her long and fruitful ministry.

Demonstrating Leadership Qualities

Of course, there can be many more leadership qualities beyond these twelve, depending on circumstances. However, these twelve essential qualities address requirements for leaders in most direct contact contexts as well as at high levels. And the higher the level of leadership and the broader the scope for which a person is responsible, the more each of the aforementioned qualities is necessary.

Some leaders have a limited span of responsibility; they may not have to demonstrate all twelve. For example, a supervisor of a crew of laborers is going to be more effective with good leadership skills. But he is not likely to have to demonstrate a great amount of foresight or influence in that role, whereas a CEO definitely will. At the CEO level, it is probable that every one of the qualities described will be critical. And leaders at high levels must be *continually* aware of what is important to demonstrate in their leadership role. But it takes more than being aware of what is important to do. It takes the *willingness* to do it. Sometimes that can be very challenging and often uncomfortable.

During his five-year tenure as CEO of Health Alliance Plan of Michigan, William R. Alvin helped increase membership, boosted profitability, and improved employee satisfaction. I asked Alvin about what was required to guide the business toward such positive gains. He mentioned many issues that helped to achieve those results. However, what stood out most was his emphasis upon integrity and the courage to do what was *right* versus what was convenient. Such considerations as convenience, political influences, or self gain were irrelevant to him, as they are with all principle-based leaders. However, that required not only knowing what leadership actions were most relevant to each circumstance but *taking the necessary action.*

When discussing the integrity and courage required to be an effective CEO in his organization, Alvin cited the necessity of taking action to correct a few negative practices, including how a few well-entrenched executives and managers treated others in the company. Some of the colleagues he had to contend with in correcting negative influences held powerful positions and had influence with key members on the board of directors. The stance Alvin took in the face of a few well entrenched executives put his position at risk. However, he was successful in affecting the changes necessary, which ultimately had a positive influence upon the culture at large in the company. And these changes promoted a higher emphasis on excellence as well as member service.

I asked Alvin what had been most instructive as he learned how to lead effectively. He referenced the importance of a leader's values. When questioned who was most influential on his values and where he learned about leadership, as with many outstanding leaders, he named his parents. He placed special emphasis on how they modeled characteristics that are at the core of what is necessary for a leader to build respect.

As illustrated by the experiences of Alvin, as well as other principle-based leaders, an effective leader is more a product of what they are *about* than what they have done or how popular they might be. The values and qualities of excellent leadership are the foundation of what guides their behavior. What leaders *do* to demonstrate effective leadership carries much more influence than their outward appearance, credentials, or political skills.

Taken together, the qualities referenced define leaders who are genuinely *focused upon the interests of others above their own.* They define leaders who build commitment in others based upon the most foundational building blocks of human relationships such as respect, trust, and authenticity. Additionally, such leaders think clearly and rationally, and they solve problems and identify paths to success for themselves and others. They understand and demonstrate that they must first master themselves in order to successfully lead and manage the activities of others.

Chapter 2 Summary

- *Direct contact contexts* are where most leadership skills are demonstrated.
- Regardless of the context, the one quality absolutely essential in order to lead is *influence.*
- Leaders who demonstrate *well-founded confidence* are much more likely to exercise significant influence with others.
- Effective leaders, while alert to potential loss, *do not allow themselves to be intimidated by the fear of failure* or making a mistake.
- No one is a true leader unless those they lead believe they will be *listened to.*

- Principle-based leaders demonstrate admirable *self-discipline* through their presence, behavior, and values.
- *What leaders do* to demonstrate effective leadership evokes much more positive influence than their outward appearance, their credentials, or their level of authority.

Assessment Exercise #1

A self-rating of the twelve leadership qualities described in chapter 2 is available at GreenbrierLeadership.com. On the home page, click on the blue tab titled "Additional Assessments" and then select the box titled "Universal Leadership Qualities Assessment." You can print out the assessment. After completing it, save the results for application as will be instructed in chapter 10 of this book.

CHAPTER 3

DEVELOPING LEADERSHIP QUALITIES AND SKILLS

Planning to become better at anything is enhanced by *definiteness of purpose*. A clear vision with a strong desire for success is essential. But as with any significant goal it must be backed by persistence to be sustained through whatever difficulties or setbacks may occur. Persistence is the hallmark of all major achievements. This is particularly true in respect to becoming better at leading others.

Generally, before planning to work on strengthening one's ability to lead, a few primary inquires should be conducted, regardless of the level of one's leadership experience and abilities. They are

- self-assessment of existing leadership qualities, skills, and developmental needs;
- analysis of specific situational requirements of the leadership role;
- determination of the perceived needs and goals of others the leader will affect; and
- an objective assessment of one's most natural leadership style.

Self-Assessment

As referenced in chapters 1 and 2, leadership roles and requirements often vary significantly. And obviously skills and developmental needs vary from person to person. Also, the less experienced leaders are, the more difficult it is to know what leadership skills they will find of most value in the future.

However, as described in chapter 2, there are universal leadership qualities and skills that are likely to apply across most leadership roles, whether they are formal or informal. The self-rating exercise at the end of chapter 2 may help you identify areas you should begin to focus upon. Choosing a few of the most pressing needs as identified in the assessment, with advice from a knowledgeable mentor or advisor, can be a good starting point.

Almost everyone has some potential leadership qualities. Objective knowledge of your existing leadership strengths is important, because they may then be used more effectively when called upon, depending on the need.[24] Some leadership development experts actually think it more important to identify existing skills and strengths than weaknesses, because they provide more of a solid base upon which to build. Both are important. When certain areas are deficient, it is necessary to identify them as soon as possible and begin working on improvement, as that is what enables you to more completely develop and strengthen your leadership ability overall.

The universal leadership qualities assessment illustrates that some areas are a higher priority for improvement before others. After you identify such areas that require work, you can begin improvement. Keep in mind that a *comprehensive and objective* perspective of near-term developmental needs is the first step in learning to lead more effectively.

Analyzing Specific Situational Requirements of the Leadership Role

The specific requirements of each leadership situation define what the leader must do to perform effectively. The concept of situational leadership was originally popularized by Paul Hersey and Ken Blanchard in their book on organizational behavior, *Management of Organizational Behavior*.[25]

They termed their collaborative theory "situational leadership" because it emphasizes the importance of leaders learning to analyze different variables related to situations and assess individual team members' needs. Effective leaders must *flex and adapt* their style to the unique requirements of the person they are working with or the circumstances they face. The most important variable in the process is for leaders to learn to use an approach based on the team member's individual needs.

In respect to individual team members, situational leadership suggests leaders pay close attention to at least two important variables for each person within their span of authority. One variable addresses the team member's level of competence. The other variable has to do with the amount of commitment the person demonstrates. Leaders then flex their leadership style to best fit the requirements of each individual.

For example, people with high competence and commitment usually require a different leadership style than those with low competence but high commitment. Those high on both variables will need a less directive approach, as they already know what to do and will likely do it without much prompting. People who are low on competence but high on commitment may need more directive attention from the leader until they learn enough to become fully competent in their position. Varying degrees of both variables necessitate varying styles applied by the leader to best fit the situation.[26]

Determining the Needs and Goals of Others the Leader will Effect

Understanding and becoming alert to the needs of others is a significant tool in strengthening your leadership skills. This includes needs such as rewards and work setting requirements of each individual important for them to perform well and be satisfied with their role. Working with, influencing, serving, and helping others attain their goals and needs is a central requirement of effective leadership. This is especially true with principle-based leadership, which is highly focused upon service to others. Learning how to best serve and assist others as well as understanding their wants and needs helps leaders encourage better performance.

As illustrated by many of the leaders profiled in chapter 1, a leader must have a well-founded perspective of what motivates others in order to build the commitment necessary to lead effectively. The leader may then work to ensure that the vision or paths to success are clear. Even within informal leadership contexts, people demonstrating leadership in a group setting must understand what is likely to have real value to increase the chances their suggestions, solutions, or ideas may best yield value for others.

An Objective Assessment of One's Most Natural Leadership Style

Style embodies *how* leadership is exercised. There is no limit to the number of unique leadership styles that may be identified.[27] They describe not only how involved a leader is with team members but other things unique to the leader's personality and behavior pattern. Examples of a few common categories of style include directive, supportive, collaborative, creative, consensus, perfectionist, or enabling.

> *Effective leaders must flex and adapt their style to the unique requirements of the person they are working with or the circumstances they face.*

Of course, individual leaders usually display a combination of varying degrees of a number of styles, and that is what makes every leader unique. But usually, one particular style is dominant. It is essential that effective leaders see themselves objectively, identify their most natural style, and understand how to adapt to various leadership contexts as necessary.

Leaders do not need to try to completely change their natural style, as it is unlikely that they will be able to do so for long. But they do need to know when their leadership style is effective and when it is not suitable. They may then respond to a specific situation by complimenting their natural tendencies with additional behaviors as required. However, the process of flexing styles, as well as the overall development of leadership abilities, is unusually challenging.

What Makes Learning to Become a Better Leader so Challenging?

Learning can be a function of experience, study, introspection, guidance, or any of a number of vehicles. But the learning of a sophisticated skill such as leadership is best achieved by practical experience, with a continuous focus upon becoming better. It requires much more than conceptual awareness. It requires practice.

People begin learning in infancy. Some researchers even posit that a baby in the womb can learn.[28] Therefore, the majority of the knowledge guiding behavior is cumulative, stored for future access as necessary. Because of that fact, learning new things often requires reprogramming or unlearning existing patterns. This requires focused concentration, coupled with rewards to reinforce the new knowledge or skill. And as with most learning, it often requires overriding certain habits and ways of acting that were established earlier.

Therefore, learning sophisticated new skills and behaviors entails challenges that far exceed simply hearing or reading about a better way to do something. It often actually requires reprogramming one's thinking and behavior patterns. In his outstanding work *Thinking Fast and Slow*,[29] Dr. Daniel Kahneman provides a detailed and highly engaging discourse on many facets of how the brain functions and processes information. Much of his work sheds light upon how we learn.

Dr. Kahneman maintains that there are two different but connected functions guiding behavior. One is instantaneous processing and response to stimuli. This is the "fast thinking" function, which he refers to as "System One." It is automatic and is often tied to emotions as well as deeply ingrained behavior patterns. An example would be an automatic grimace that follows an unexpected insult.

"System Two" is the function of thinking deliberately and slowly about something. An example would be the financial computations needed to choose between two vacation destinations. In the case of both fast thinking and slow thinking, the thought processes involved are deeply engrained and not easily displaced or unlearned. The fast thinking process is very much without conscious effort and for the most part routine. The slow thinking process, while deliberate, is still in large part a deeply programmed function. And in fact, Dr. Kahneman maintains that it is also very much influenced by System One, which can operate at a subconscious level.

In the System One case, a facial expression may occur automatically (unless the person has practiced learning not to telegraph negative emotions easily). In the System Two case, the automatic learned application of *how* the costs are computed will again not be replaced unless a better technique for computing them is acquired. But obviously, both fast thinking and slow thinking are in large part habitual and therefore deeply embedded.

Dr. Kahneman's research indicates that the way the human brain functions is highly complex and to reprogram it by acquiring appropriate new skills and behaviors requires much focus and disciplined effort. This is especially true when endeavoring to become a better leader, including learning how to make better decisions, use better judgment, and improve interactions with others.

All self-development efforts, whether physical, educational, or practical, such as learning to develop one's leadership ability, are usually best achieved with the help and encouragement of others. However, the ultimate responsibility rests within yourself. Your growth on the leadership continuum should never end, it should be a lifelong pursuit. It is best achieved with a logical and well-planned approach for learning. And to ensure that learning has practical and lasting value, a number of considerations must be addressed along the way.

What Is Necessary to Ensure that Learning a New Skill Will Be Lasting?

There are five essential steps that must be addressed in changing behavior or learning a new skill that will stay with the learner for the long term. The first step is having a good *reason* to learn the skill or change the behavior to begin with. If there is no practical reason to learn something new or change behavior, it's likely to be discarded or forgotten soon after, as it will prove to have no real value.

> *Learning sophisticated new skills and behaviors entails challenges that far exceed simply hearing or reading about a better way to do something.*

Next, learners must identify a particular skill or behavior that is likely to have value and *believe there is good reason for learning it*. If they don't, there is little chance they will invest the amount of effort and practice required to apply the skill. The information may be gained by attending a seminar, receiving coaching, or completing a book, an online course, or video-based training program. But that is usually not enough to effect long-term behavior change. However, that is too often where the process stops. Too many people sign up for a seminar or class, or read a popular book and then quickly forget or never use the information after completion of the program.

Third, the learning must be *used* or *practiced*. It's not enough to know conceptually how to do something. Learning how to do something does not automatically translate to doing it when the time comes. If the techniques involved in the learning exercises are not practiced correctly and regularly, there will be no positive results, and they will soon be lost or forgotten.

Having a good reason for learning a new skill, conceptual learning, and then practicing the new skill is still not likely to produce mastery without two additional steps. The fourth essential step is the *visualization* of success. Learners must continue to believe they will become better and visualize what success looks like. They must keep focused upon the rewards that the learning will yield. Without that, they may not be able to sustain the amount of effort long enough to allow the new behavior to become automatic.

Finally, to ensure that the new skill or behavior becomes automatic, one more ingredient is needed. That ingredient is *success*. There must be reinforcement to solidify the new technique, skill, or ability.

All five of the steps required for changing behavior are especially relevant to becoming a better leader. This is because so much of leadership is based upon human interaction, which is often automatic. For instance, if supervisors attempt to improve their listening skills to develop more leadership presence and capability, it will take more than simply attending a seminar on listening skills. They will have to find a way to actually apply techniques from the program back in the work setting, often enough to make it a natural part of their work with others. And of course, there must be some level of value and success to ensure that they continue to use the new techniques.

Requirements to Ensure a New Skill Will Be Lasting

✓ A good reason to learn a new skill or change behavior to begin with

✓ Identification of a particular skill or behavior that is likely to have value and believing there is good reason for learning it

✓ The learning must be used or practiced in a regular and disciplined fashion

✓ Visualization and expectation of success with the new skill or behavior

✓ Success that will reinforce the learning to ensure it becomes automatic

How Can I Best Plan My Growth on Building Leadership Skills?

To increase the likelihood that real growth will result while learning to strengthen leadership qualities, each of the following requirements should be considered:

1. *Establish realistic goals*

Unless a goal is *realistic* and will yield practical value, it's unlikely the effort to achieve it will prove successful. For example, if a person sets a goal of completing medical school to become a pediatrician, but they do not have the requisite academic skills, the goal probably will not result in success, no matter how much effort is expended.

In the case of leadership, the goal must specify the kind of leadership skill necessary to fulfill the proper context and role. And that requires asking the right questions about yourself, including what you are capable of and what is worth doing. Well-conceived questions and answers about yourself should be based upon an objective evaluation of your current strengths and weaknesses, your long-term aspirations, and the kinds of leadership contexts you are most likely to find yourself participating in.

In respect to your current capabilities, these include existing skills and abilities, knowledge level, potential talents, initiative, and related personal assets. Perhaps most important is identifying what leadership qualities are most worth acquiring in respect to your long-term plans. They may be to enhance existing qualities and strengths or to identify and develop brand new skills to complement your existing strengths. But they must be realistic and specified.

Gaining objective and informed feedback as well as advice from people who know you is invaluable. Seek feedback from as many sources as are practical. Pay closest attention to information from highly knowledgeable and objective parties who are well acquainted with you. Avoid discouragement, but embrace constructive critiques.

Encourage constructive criticism as often as practical. Don't let the fear of criticism inhibit your desire to become better.

> *There is only one way to avoid criticism: do nothing; say nothing; and be nothing.* —Aristotle

Tie your leadership development goals into your vision of your future as well as what is most meaningful and rewarding to you. Keep in mind that any worthwhile goal to develop the self is largely a function of positive expectations. What a person thinks about their potential for success actually does influence the likelihood of success. Theory and research on autosuggestion[30] suggests that everything a person thinks consciously will ultimately influence the outcomes of their goals. Consider what you hope to achieve in the long run. Keep in mind that there is no asset greater than excellent leadership skills to open the doors to opportunity. The stronger your leadership abilities, the more likely you will experience fulfillment and success in both your professional as well as your personal life.

2. *Identify Effective Methods of Self-Development that Most Suit Your Needs*

Your selected methods for leadership development have to be practical and doable to be worth the time and effort you expend. Similar to a well-conceived goal, the methods must fit the capabilities of the individual while ensuring personal growth toward an achievable and worthwhile goal in a specific context. The focus of your leadership goals should be upon acquiring the specific behaviors and skills that will most likely result in tangible value.

In the case of leadership, this means the method must not only foster awareness of how to become better at a particular leadership skill, it must also identify the explicit activities that will actually result in improved leadership. For instance, if you want to strengthen your ability to build teamwork in groups, you need a practical setting to apply the activities that will enable you to actually observe what works best in groups.

Learning to become a better leader means *changing* behavior. Acquiring any new skill or ability requires learning to adopt different and more effective ways of doing some things and discarding other behaviors. Because most existing behaviors are automatic, it may take quite a bit of work to override them. For example, acquiring the ability to hit a tennis ball skillfully requires many hours of practice learning to coordinate the timing, muscle movements, balance, and numerous other actions until the action becomes automatic. But that will require discontinuing automatic behaviors that interfere with correct form. It must be mastered to the point that little thought is necessary to ensure the proper action.

3. *Plan to Sustain Disciplined Effort over Time*

As emphasized previously, significant and worthwhile personal growth is never simple or easy. Not only does it often involve sacrifice and some level of discomfort, it also requires hard work, typically over a long enough period that the new skills become well established and automatic. This is especially true in the context of leadership, which deals with the complex domain of human dynamics. There are usually no quick or easy ways to strengthen your ability to work with or influence others positively, as an effective leader must do.

Opportunities to practice applying leadership skills do not always present themselves at convenient times. As a result, leaders must remain continually vigilant and alert for chances to apply good principles of leadership at the moment they occur. One way they may increase the likelihood of making sure they are alert to such opportunities is to identify specific people or groups who would benefit from improved leadership influence. Then the leader must be flexible enough to capitalize upon opportunities when they present themselves.

4.   *Ongoing Evaluation and Growth*

Learning to become a better leader is not a specific end; it is a continuing evolution of the person. It requires that the leader identify objective ways to evaluate what works best, determine what isn't working, and recognize additional paths for development to ensure continuing growth.

Evaluation of progress on learning to lead more effectively is best determined by analysis of specific results. This requires objective scrutiny of outcomes from application of newly acquired techniques, skills, approaches, and strategies. It is important to put aside emotions and personal subjective feelings when evaluating the outcomes. To be worthwhile, evaluation needs to focus upon rational analysis of what occurred, why it occurred, and how it may be improved.

Additionally, seeking informed feedback from others is essential to gaining a broad and balanced perspective on progress as well as continuing to look for areas to focus upon. The feedback may come from people you describe the circumstances to or others who actually observed it firsthand. But regardless, that feedback should come from others who are objective and knowledgeable enough to present informed counsel.

What Are the Best Resources for Developing Leadership?

The most worthwhile self-development begins with individuals deciding to take personal responsibility for their own growth and success. It cannot be abdicated to anyone else. *Ultimately, each of us is most responsible for what we become, achieve, and contribute.* This is particularly true when developing leadership skills, because this is primarily a function driven by self-initiative.

Because leadership is unexcelled in respect to its potential to facilitate pursuit of a meaningful life as well as improve the lives of others, the ability to lead effectively has unequaled value for establishing purpose whether professional, personal, or in other respects. Self-responsibility as exercised through self-driven efforts in leadership development is the foundation upon which principle-based leadership is based.

Once leaders develop goals for strengthening their leadership on dimensions they ascertain as necessary for success, they can identify the most practical and effective resources through which to learn. Experience is the best teacher. But experience in leadership roles may not avail itself easily. Additionally, it may be better to learn about what to do before attempting the trial-and-error method that so often characterizes doing something for the first time. When possible, it is often best to learn about things conceptually, if practical, before doing them, as that may heighten the value of the real world experience when it occurs.

Importantly, experience is more likely to be the best teacher when the learner is sharp enough to acquire the knowledge the first time around.

> *Experience is the best teacher but a fool will learn from no other.*—Ben Franklin

Studies and Formal Programs

Learning about leadership methods, techniques, and successful leaders has value, to an extent. The value is to make students more aware of the subject conceptually, which will enable them to learn quickly and more effectively from practical lessons such as is afforded by practical experience.

Reading biographies about successful leaders, studying why leaders are successful, and related approaches usually have much more value if the student can discuss the lessons with others. This is why many excellent schools of leadership, such as the Wharton School, the Center for Creative Leadership, and the Stanford Center for

Leadership, use learning labs and group discussions as core tools in their programs. Students undertaking a self-study program for strengthening their leadership are best advised to discuss what they are learning with others, particularly peers or others who have practical leadership experience. Appendix B includes a list of excellent resources to supplement the information we will be addressing.

Online Resources

Free or relatively inexpensive online programs on the subject of leadership are plentiful on the Internet. Like books or courses, this is an excellent way to become exposed to concepts of leadership and learn more about how to develop improved leadership

> *The most worthwhile self-development begins with individuals deciding to take personal responsibility for their own growth and success.*

skills. While nothing replaces real life experience, many online sources on leadership development are outstanding preparation when done in conjunction with practical application. A number of such excellent sources are also included in Appendix B.

Modeling

Another excellent method for learning about leadership, modeling, is observing others who are effective and studying why they are effective.[31] This is one of the best methods for learning any human interactive skill but particularly so with leadership. In this case, the learner is afforded the opportunity to observe firsthand what works as well as what does not work and the outcomes of various behaviors and activities demonstrated in practical contexts.

Modeling, is heightened if the learner is fortunate enough to work closely with the model. This is why highly respected professionals who exercise leadership, whether in business, coaching, or teaching, are sought out by understudies. It's no coincidence that football coaching greats like Paul "Bear" Bryant of Alabama and Vince Lombardi of the Green Bay Packers have had so many former assistants go on to become successful coaches.

Mentoring

Being personally mentored by a successful leader is unexcelled for strengthening leadership abilities.[32] Many leadership development experts believe it is the absolute best method to learn how to become a more effective leader. Not only does it have all the benefits of modeling, learners also receive focused development attention and feedback that is keyed directly to their specific needs and goals.

A strong mentoring relationship is built on collaboration and the commitment of the mentor to the professional development of the person to be mentored. In most mentoring relationships, the senior participant typically has more experience, skill, and knowledge than the person being mentored. But many strong mentoring relationships provide an opportunity for both parties to learn from each other through the development of a mutually beneficial partnership, in which leadership challenges and issues are discussed openly and constructively.

Putting It All Together

Each of the learning methods we have referenced has significant value for development of leadership abilities. The best approach may be using some of each, if the learner is afforded the opportunity to participate in such a broad learning environment. Because effective leaders never really stop learning how to be better, it is likely they will continue to participate in all forms available to them as long as they live.

Unquestionably, one of the most essential qualities of people who become outstanding leaders is that they are open to valid critique and input from others. Ultimately, leaders are only as effective as the results they produce in the interest of those they lead. Because of this, leaders must be closely in touch with the feelings, perspectives, and inputs of those they lead to really know how they are doing and how to continue to improve. If possible, they should continually seek honest appraisals from all sources, including those they lead, for as long as they intend to remain in a leadership role.

Chapter 3 Summary

- Identifying specific *qualities and skills* for development relevant to your actual leadership role significantly increases your likelihood of success.
- Learning about leadership demands much more than conceptual awareness; it requires *practice.*
- Learning to become a better leader often requires *reprogramming* your thinking and behavior patterns in a number of contexts keyed to your leadership role.
- The stronger your leadership abilities, the more likely you will experience fulfillment and success in both your professional as well as your personal life.
- Developing leadership skills is most successful when driven by strong *self-initiative.*
- Being personally *mentored* by a successful leader is unexcelled for strengthening leadership abilities.
- Ultimately, leaders are only as effective as the results they produce in the interest of those they lead.

Assessment Exercise #2

Chapter 4 addresses leadership styles and you will obtain much more value from the chapter by participating in a leadership style self-assessment. Go to the GreenbrierLeadership.com homepage and click on the blue "Leadership Style Assessment" tab to participate in a short style assessment. You will be directed to select from twenty sets of four descriptive terms about yourself. Choose the term that is most like you in your current leadership role or work setting. Then click on "Finish" to receive your evaluation. You may then click on the "Print" icon to produce a full hard copy of the results. You will need that assessment in chapter 10.

CHAPTER 4

LEADERSHIP STYLES

As illustrated by exercise 2 at the end of chapter 3, leadership style has to do with *how* we lead. It embodies the manner for interacting with others, such as from directive to supportive or from perfectionist to spontaneous. Style assessments can describe how a person manages their job or area of responsibility such as the level of priority established for people versus production tradeoffs.[33] It can include any of a number of different dimensions that describe how a person leads depending upon what it is designed to assess but normally, there are one or two dimensions that are dominant in each person's style.

What we do to lead is very much influenced by our style. The "what" includes the specific behaviors and activities chosen or applied during functions like interactions, making decisions, and other requirements of the leader's role. We will address the behavioral side of leadership in chapter 5. Style then shapes how we perform the behaviors through which we exercise leadership.

For example, a leader with a highly perfectionist style is likely to apply much preparation before reviewing an employee's work on a project, whereas a leader with a highly spontaneous style may pay less attention to preparation and just begin the review in an open-ended discussion format, asking the employee how he or she is doing. Each leader's style influences specifically how the review is conducted.

When leaders have a firm understanding of their most natural style and the way it influences how they interact and exercise leadership, they are likely to be more effective. It's an advantage for leaders to be aware of a variety of appropriate style considerations that best apply for the persons they lead and the situation at hand. This increases their flexibility to make adjustments and lead more effectively.

How Does a Person's Leadership Style Influence the Way Others React to Them?

People usually react to leaders as a result of how they perceive the leader's role, personality, and influence. Because of that fact, the more we know about how we are perceived by others, the more successfully we can work with others. This is particularly so with leaders, because their success is contingent upon the influence they exert on others. As leaders gain an objective understanding of how their behavior affects the behavior and feelings of others, they are better prepared to know what to do to have value and lead more effectively.

The manner in which leaders engage with others in direct contact contexts and exercise their role influences the nature of the dynamic between the leader and the team. People around the leader naturally form a notion of what the leader is all about and how they are most likely to behave. If leaders have an objective and accurate view of how they are perceived, they are much more likely to use that information to strengthen their leadership behavior.

It's not possible to name every conceivable continuum of leadership style and behavior, as every leader has specific facets that are unique to them, the same as their facial appearance and personality. However, it is possible to identify basic categories of leadership style and place leaders in one that describes much of the behavior they are likely to demonstrate.

If we were to identify two basic categories of leadership on a continuum as "supportive" at one end and "directive" at the other, it would not be difficult to define what kinds of behaviors attend each end of the continuum. Supportive would include careful listening and encouraging. Directive would include providing specific guidelines on what must be accomplished as well as the standards that must be met.

Having that continuum and then examining the behavior of a certain leader, we could at the least be able to determine which end of the continuum they are closer to. Then if we had to, we could assign each leader in a category of supportive style or directive style. While that would not describe all of their leadership profile, it would help us and the leader know some common types of behaviors we may expect in certain contexts. No one style is necessarily any better than another, overall. However, depending upon the circumstance, one style might better suit the leadership needs of the situation than would another.

> *The more we know about how we are genuinely perceived by others, the more successfully we can work with them.*

Leaders who know that they are perceived as directive and understand that this is their common disposition may then work to complement that type of behavior when necessary. However, if they have little or no awareness that they are perceived as directive, that could work against them (for example, if they are unaware of the need to demonstrate less directive behavior and more flexibility).

What's the Difference between Leadership Style and Personality Style?

Both contexts have to do with many of the same considerations. Both may address how a person behaves, including interacting with others, listening and speaking, initiating actions in work settings, assisting others, and other common dynamics with people. Additionally, both may address how the person conducts non-interactive behaviors such as the amount of detail focus demonstrated on work tasks, how time is managed, and other deeply conditioned habits of behavior.

The difference is simply that leadership style is a subset of personality style. It focuses more upon the narrower context of common natural behavior in leadership roles. More specifically, it describes likely personality traits and behaviors when the person is functioning in a formal or informal leadership role. Leadership style is the natural behavior that will occur most often in leadership roles unless the leader makes a conscious decision to override or flex the behavior.

Broad personality style assessments cover additional areas beyond the leadership context, such as interaction with others outside of work settings, socially, with family, or related contexts. Leadership style assessments then focus upon what the subject will most probably do in leadership roles. And this may not be the same thing they will do outside leadership roles.

In fact, many classical type indicators, such as the Myers-Briggs or the DISC profile, have excellent utility in predicting behavior of subjects in leadership roles. These very accurate type indicators address a broad array of common behaviors across a number of potentially different contexts in which the subject may participate, including leadership.

But there is at least one important difference between using an assessment defined as a leadership style assessment and using one of the other broader context personality indicators. It is that the leadership style assessment generally limits its applicability to leadership role considerations. Activities such as delegation, supervision, creativity, influence, and related leadership requirements generally receive more focus and attention during the interpretation and application of leadership style assessments.

Is It Possible for a Person to Change Their Natural Leadership Style?

Because natural behavior is driven by a combination of hereditary traits and the habits people adopt over their lives, it is largely unconscious or automatic. The behavior is done without the person having to think much about it, if at all. Both "nature," the inherent characteristics programmed genetically, and "nurture," the events in life that condition and reinforce certain behaviors, are always at work subconsciously. Because of that deep programming, people cannot make much significant change in their natural behavior without a significant amount of focus and work.

However, when leaders are aware of their natural personality type or leadership style, they may be much more alert to determine how to either capitalize on their style or complement their style, depending upon the situation. This is classic situational leadership. Effective leaders think about what is happening and deliberately flex their approach to best fit the circumstance.

For example, Barb recognizes that assertive and quick acting behaviors are a natural part of her leadership style. She may recognize that she tends to be more impatient than patient. Let's suppose she finds herself in a leadership context that requires her to be more patient and slower acting. *If she is aware* of her tendency to act more quickly than the circumstance requires, she might override her natural tendency and handle the situation more deliberately. That may result in Barb handling it much more effectively. So when she is consciously aware of her most natural tendencies to begin with, she may know how to better manage herself as necessary to improve results. This is why participating in a leadership style assessment may have value for her. It can make her much more aware of her most natural tendencies and where she should flex her style as necessary.

In another case, Dewayne's leadership style is tolerant and not focused on tasks. Much of his behavior is characterized by reaction instead of action. He is not aware of this fact and isn't alert to where that style may not be appropriate. If he finds himself

> *Because natural behavior is driven by a combination of hereditary traits and the habits people adopt over their lives, it is largely unconscious and automatic.*

leading a team that lacks focus, has low quality standards, and is unable to complete projects on time, he might have some serious challenges to lead the team effectively. Unless he can complement his usual style of leadership with behaviors that will raise expectations as well as promote much greater accountability, it is not likely his team will change much for the better.

So while leaders may not be able to change their *natural inclination* to behave in a certain manner, they can learn to flex their most natural styles when necessary in ways that will allow them to be more effective. Some historical leaders best known for their style demonstrated radical departures from what was normally expected of them.

General George Patton, the famous WWII commander, was nicknamed "Old Blood and Guts" because of his hard core demeanor and behavior. However, after a couple of infamous instances of using a heavy-handed approach with his soldiers, the general knew it would be best to apologize, even though that was totally out of character for him.[34] General Patton did ultimately humble himself and apologize to the soldiers, as well as his troops, in an emotional speech. He knew it was not only warranted but necessary to demonstrate respect and compassion for his men.

How Can Leadership Style Information Be Used to Improve Leadership Capabilities?

The ability to adapt to various situational requirements, as well as different personalities of team members, is essential for effective leadership in direct contact contexts. Leaders who have a framework for recognizing personality differences or similarities between themselves and their team members have a distinct advantage to communicate and lead more successfully. Their self-management capabilities increase exponentially. They are better prepared to resolve conflict. They are better able to develop rapport. And they are better equipped to encourage positive team dynamics.

The following are important considerations related to knowledge of leadership styles as well as differing styles of team members:

- **_Capitalizing on strengths_**

When leaders have an objective and systematic assessment profile of their leadership style, they are in a better position to capitalize upon their strengths. Such information provides a framework for establishing what strengths may be used to be more effective and how they can be applied most practically. And importantly, leaders will have an objective view of which areas are not their strengths. In that case, they may either work to improve their ability in such areas or compensate where possible.

For example, let's consider the case of a leader whose assessment reveals strengths in promotional ability but low emphasis on follow through. It that case, she knows that to be more effective, she will either have to pay special attention to setting goals with time frames or identify someone on her team who can help ensure she stays on task. In some cases, she may delegate follow through to a team member, if it is appropriate. However, it is best for leaders to try to pull up their skills in areas that are deficient, if it is practical. This is especially true in respect to interactive activities such as communications and developing team members.

- **_Gaining perspective upon how others are likely to perceive leaders based upon their style_**

One of the more challenging tasks leaders face is to see themselves objectively. It's difficult for many persons in leadership positions to have accurate perspective of how they are regarded or perceived by others. There are a number of reasons for this fact. It may be due to the normal inclination for people to not tell their supervisors exactly how they feel about them. Regardless, the more objective and valid information leaders can gain upon how others are inclined to react to their style, the more informed they are about how to best capitalize on their style or complement it. When leaders receive valid information on their style from an assessment, they can use the information to improve how they lead.

- ### *Improving approaches for communicating with team members*

Differing personality styles may sometimes have extra challenges in communicating with one another. This is not necessarily true in all cases, but it often is. For example, if a leader has an outgoing style and a team member is introverted and possibly a little intimidated by outgoing types, the leader may need to relax somewhat with that person. That may increase the comfort level between both parties and make communications a little easier. The more familiar leaders are with a basic understanding and knowledge about the communications needs of the styles of others, the better for communicating with them in ways that will more likely promote rapport and understanding.

- ### *Anticipating how team members may interpret leaders' actions as a function of their style*

Leaders are communicating more by their actions than their words. An often quoted phrase, "Your actions are speaking so loudly I can't hear what you are saying," makes the point. As a result, many times leaders do not have an opportunity to tell team members why they are doing something or even what they are intending to do. Because leaders are normally in a higher position of visibility than team members, they need to consider how their actions may be interpreted. Often their style may evoke assumptions by others that may need to be considered. This is particularly true if team members don't understand how significant a person's style is in shaping their behavior.

Some leaders offer their team members the opportunity to participate in style assessment exercises together and share results.

This enables each team member to understand differences in how others behave as a function of their unique style characteristics. Such exercises may promote heightened understanding and acceptance of the differences of others. However, such exercises should be handled carefully by skilled practitioners and only involve team members who are open to and comfortable with such interventions.

- *Knowing what is likely to make various styles comfortable or uncomfortable in work settings*

The more knowledgeable leaders are about the differences in communications needs as well as work setting requirements of different styles, the better equipped they are to promote positive dynamics between themselves and team members. And of course, leaders may then complement their most natural behaviors to promote greater harmony on the team.

Objective and accurate knowledge on each of the aforementioned variables enables leaders to vary their approach to increase their influence and achieve results. This does not require leaders to change their standards or their goals. And they should not try to change themselves. But they must be flexible and adapt to various style requirements when appropriate and practical. Ultimately, it is the leader who must assume the principle responsibility for promoting harmony and good communications on the team.

What is the best overall leadership style that has the greatest value in most settings?

There is no "best" leadership style. Regardless of style, leaders will be highly effective only if they lead others to successful results. That usually requires that they are knowledgeable and competent in their leadership context; others respect them and want to follow their leadership; they can handle whatever risks arise; and they make good decisions. None of those attributes are exclusive to any specific leadership style.

However, as discussed, good leaders know how to flex their style in response to various situations. In fact, the ability to be flexible is more important in being a successful leader than any particular style. While it is true that in certain situations, a direct and task-oriented style may be required, while a deliberate and careful style may be best in another, it is not likely that any leadership role requires one type of style for every situation. Even a Marine Corps drill instructor must depart from the traditional forceful style from time to time to encourage or even support certain soldiers in boot camp.

It is often good for persons new to leadership roles to pay careful attention to how others above or beside them lead. The new leader may observe certain approaches that work well and consider adopting those approaches when appropriate. They may observe other approaches that they decide they want to avoid. In essence, they are learning by identifying specific leadership behaviors that are effective and behaviors that they want to avoid. This can often best be learned as a function of careful examination of how others lead. Again, this requires deliberate thought and flexibility to use the best approach to address the circumstances at hand.

Is It Appropriate to Use Style Information to Select Team Members?

If a leader is hiring a new team member (or selecting new members from a different group), it is important to outline the knowledge, skills, and abilities necessary to do the job. If there is a significant learning curve, obviously the ability to learn the job will be critical. If new team members have to be skilled to begin with, they must come in with enough knowledge to perform with competence quickly. In addition, the leader will hope to hire someone who fits the culture and is motivated by the available rewards.

However, a personality assessment is not normally a good indicator of any of the aforementioned selection criteria. In fact, attempting to use personality type indicators as selection instruments usually ignores many important requirements for new hires. This is because regardless of a person's personality style, they will fit a culture as a function of how they relate to and work with others. And that is not the specific province of any particular style. Their attitude toward their work and interest in getting along with others, combined with their level of potential competence, will carry far more weight in predicting their fit to the team. Too often, hiring managers try to use personality type assessments and base hiring decisions on considerations that are not especially relevant or appropriate for new hires.

How Do Roles Influence the Leadership Dynamic?

Leadership style, just like personality style, is an important dimension for understanding why people behave the way they do and for predicting behavior. However, style information is rarely enough by itself to make important decisions on working with or interacting with others. Too often some psychologists and management consultants place almost exclusive emphasize upon using personality assessments to counsel, coach, or build team effectiveness.

Regardless of a person's most dominant characteristics, as demonstrated in their style, there are other important variables that will affect how they actually behave in any given instance. One is the role the person *believes* they should play. By "role," we are referring to the responsibilities a person assumes and the activities they undertake. The role the person adopts may modify certain behaviors that might not be common for their most natural style.

> *Regardless of style, leaders will be effective only if they lead others to successful results.*

I emphasize "the role the person believes they should play," because often the role someone thinks they play may not in fact be the role others see them in. Their actual role may be different. For example, Fred may see himself as the quality control expert in a project group, but that might not actually be the case. Others may see him adding little value in quality control but having more value in cost control because of his finance background. However, the team leader is better informed, if he knows what role Fred thinks he is playing, whether accurate or not, in order to better provide leadership for him.

In respect to leaders, accurate assessment of their own role is obviously a crucial variable too. Let's suppose Stacy is a detail-oriented and perfectionist type leader assigned the temporary job of managing a highly creative and fast-paced marketing team. She may have to modify her style somewhat as a function of her new role. With accurate self-assessment she knows to loosen her normal high focus on details and procedures, assuming more of an enabling pattern. With objective perspective upon her natural role she may know that often during the creative process, she will have to step back and allow the team to collaborate without the level of attention to policies and procedures she usually requires. She has not changed her core style. But she has adapted to her new role requirements for at least this instance.

What Place Do Values Play in Interactions with Others?

Having an accurate perspective on the styles as well as the role everyone plays in a team is still limited without an additional important variable. This is the values scheme of each person. Values refer to *what is important*. Values may vary dramatically among team members, even if they all appear to come from the same educational background or experience. Values include not only what drives a person's level of effort but also what satisfies them. The values people carry are a function of widely varying influences.

Each person's individuality is largely a product of genetically determined characteristics as well as behaviors and interests shaped by experience. But what is important to a person is not necessarily predictable because of their background, education, or inherited characteristics. It's not uncommon for two identical twins to have very different motives. One might be motivated toward financial rewards while the other may be more interested in earning recognition.

In addition to genetically determined characteristics, life experiences have a powerful impact upon values. How a child is raised, cultural norms, life altering events, and myriad other considerations affect what a person deems important. These wide differences shape our attitude, not only on what we think is important but also on what we find desirable.

Some leaders mistakenly assume that because a person has a certain personality style, it is possible to predict their values. For example, even though a strong task-oriented and assertive personality may seem to want their own ends above all else, that is not necessarily correct. They might be far more helpful and service oriented than one would assume on first impression. Often the values of a person are not quickly or easily revealed. It usually takes time to understand what is important to individuals, and that is best determined by developing genuine and mutually respectful relationships.

There are countless dimensions to values, and a leader may never know all that goes on in the minds of the team members concerning their wants and needs. Even after years of experience and close interaction, there may be facets that are still unrevealed. However, if a leader takes the time to talk with and listen to team members about what is important to them, their values will eventually surface. During such interaction, the leader should not make assumptions about anything. It is important to take the time to discover what is important and unique about the individual. The information may help open doors for others that will provide significant incentive to achieve higher performance. Even if it does not, it helps the leader learn how to work more effectively with the individual.

When considering style, it should be placed in the context of the person's role as well as their value scheme. All three taken together provide a much clearer perspective upon why a person behaves the way they do than simply considering style alone.

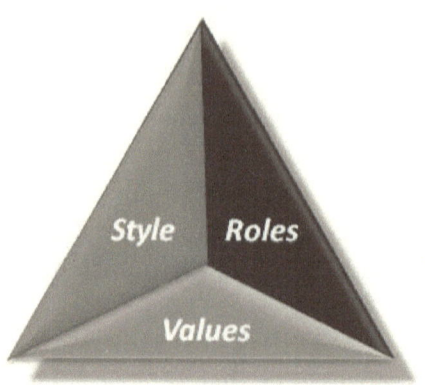

> ➤ *Style - How we interact, lead, and manage our responsibilities*
> ➤ *Roles - Our position with others and what is expected in respect to them*
> ➤ *Values - Rewards, interests and goals that are important to us as individuals*

What Role Does the Leader's Values play in the Leadership Equation?

Leaders' values eventually become obvious to team members, even if they do not describe them verbally. Actions tell much more about a person than their words. And because *Each person's individuality is largely a product of genetically determined characteristics as well as behaviors and interests shaped by experience.* leaders are in much more visible positions than others, they are continuously communicating what is important to them. They are also unconsciously communicating how they feel about others, as well as many other facts.

When leaders demonstrate their values by their actions, including respect for others, integrity, and selflessness, they won't have to try to convince anyone of the validity of their intentions by what they say. Those values will come through loud and clear very quickly. However, if they do not live up to those values, it will not matter how well they talk or how good they look; others will soon know where they stand.

This does not mean that leaders have to share the same interests, political opinions, or personal views as their team members to be effective. It does mean that they must reflect positive values that others can respect and which demonstrate their ability to generate value for others. This is an advantage resulting from principle-based leadership.

How Does a Leader Know the Best Leadership Approach for Each Individual?

Leaders can't know everything that affects the behavior of everyone within their span of responsibility. Of course, the more they know about each person's style, the role that person believes they play, and their values, the better. However, when leading with less than all the facts, leaders tend to make assumptions. This often leads to more problems than solutions.

A common mistake of many people in leadership positions is making ill-conceived assumptions. For example, leaders often mistakenly assume that the same things that are important to them are important to others in their organization. Another common mistake is basing assumptions on a person's age, gender, ethnic origin, demographics, or other characteristic. In fact, the fewer assumptions leaders have to make, the more likely they will be to lead effectively.

Effective leaders know that everyone is an individual, and they treat everyone as an individual. But this requires forming genuine relationships. Genuine relationships take longer to develop than casual or surface relationships. However, it isn't always possible for leaders to develop the level of knowledge or rapport they would prefer with each person. Regardless, it is still necessary to treat each person as an individual. This means avoiding assumptions and being open to learning as much as possible about everyone they can.

The basic guidelines established by situational leadership are a good place to begin, even if the leader knows nothing about the individual's style, role, or values. Leaders can quickly assess a person's level of competence and level of commitment, but additional information on style, role, and values is critical and can take longer. But in the meantime, when leaders know how capable and motivated a person is, they are better equipped to flex their style as necessary and lead more effectively.

Chapter 4 Summary

- Style information about the self as well as others provides leaders important perspective upon *how* to lead more effectively in all direct contact contexts.
- Leadership *style* defines what is unique to how leaders interact with others as well as manage the responsibilities of their role.
- There is no "best" leadership style for all situations; effective leaders are *flexible,* with style contingent upon the unique requirements of each situation.
- Both "nature" and "nurture," which condition and reinforce behavior, are always at work subconsciously, affecting one's style, decisions, and actions.
- Ultimately, leaders must assume the principle responsibility for promoting harmony and good communications in their span of influence.
- Others *styles,* along with *values* and *perceived roles,* are primary determinants a leader must understand to build rapport and mutual respect.

- *Values* may vary dramatically among team members, even if they all appear to come from the same educational background or experience.
- Effective leaders avoid making *assumptions* about others, when practical, by attempting to learn what makes each person unique.

Assessment Exercise #3

Chapter 5 addresses leadership behaviors; you will obtain much more value from that chapter by completing a self-rating on your own leadership behavior. Go to the GreenbrierLeadership.com homepage, click on the blue "Additional Assessments" tab, and then select "Leadership Behavior Index" (LBI). You can print out the assessment. After completing it, save the results for application in chapter 10.

You may also gain value from having someone who works closely with you complete the LBI assessment about you. However, if you choose to pursue that option, be certain that the person is well informed, objective, and comfortable discussing such information with you. Do not argue with them. Listen, ask questions, take notes, and then thank them for helping you.

CHAPTER 5

LEADERSHIP BEHAVIOR

While leadership style is *how we lead*, leadership behavior is *what we do* to lead. Ultimately, it is only what a leader *does* as opposed to what he says that makes the difference between success and failure. While style focuses upon broad categories of emphasis such as perfectionism, enabling, directive, or creative approaches, leadership behavior focuses upon the specific activities that support each of those styles through what the leader *does*.

Let's say that Courtney's leadership style can be categorized as *perfectionist*. Behavior that supports this style includes providing specific guidelines on assignments, following closely those to whom she delegates, and insisting upon high standards of performance. Depending upon the level of emphasis she applies to those specific behaviors, they may contribute to success or, with some team members, deter the effectiveness of those she leads. As is true for all leadership styles and associated strengths, overemphasis upon one's strengths, in this case perfectionism for Courtney, can turn the strength into a liability. [35]

An executive coach working with Courtney to improve her leadership may diagnose her leadership style and recommend she be more flexible. However, to better enable Courtney, there must be a focus upon specific behaviors. For example, if she overemphasizes any behavior, such as following too closely after delegating, she may actually deter performance by becoming a distraction to others. This is commonly termed "micromanagement." Citing such specific behaviors for improvement for her and the appropriate level of application provides a focus that is of much greater utility than broad or general recommendations.

Knowing specifically what to do and how to do it, the correct behavior, is often a critical variable in success, especially when leading. Jerry Stocking, author of *Cognitive Harmony: An Adventure in Mental Fitness,* emphasizes the need for sufficient focus for learning to do anything well, regardless of the subject:

> *For years humanity has been attempting to discover what makes people behave the way they do. How is it possible that when confronted with the same task or problem, two people will attempt very different means of solving it? Why do some people excel while others perform at a mediocre level? . . . Missing is the ability to discern specifically what one person is doing well and pass these skills on behaviorally to others.*[36]

Identifying the appropriate behaviors and context is frequently the key to improving performance. This challenge is particularly relevant to organizations where there is a need to strengthen leadership, because it is inadequate or missing all together. In part, this dilemma is a function of a lack of comprehending behaviorally what leaders actually must do to be successful.

John P. Kotter[37] maintains that too often those who head organizations are blind to the critical difference between behaviors that support "leading" and behaviors that support "managing." Kotter proposes that management and leadership are different but complementary skills; he says that in a changing world, one cannot function adequately without the other:

> *Managers promote stability while leaders press for change, and only organizations that embrace both sides of that contradiction can thrive in turbulent times.*

When studying leadership, and more specifically, how to develop one's own leadership skills, discerning between leadership behavior and managerial behavior is paramount to becoming a better leader. Kotter and other credible experts take the position that these terms are not interchangeable.

> *Ultimately, it is only what a leader does as opposed to what he says that makes the difference between success and failure.*

It is true that both leaders and managers must do many of the same things. Both have to communicate, make decisions, handle risk, delegate, build relationships, and solve problems to achieve goals. The primary behavior difference between leading and managing is that leadership is more about *establishing* a course. Managing is more about *executing* that course. Leaders inspire, managers control; leaders set direction, managers carry out direction; leaders promote change, managers handle complexity; leaders align people, managers organize people; leaders promote meaningful action, managers promote effective action. In essence, leadership is responsible for vision and influence. Management is responsible for maintenance and control.

Neither role can be absolutely exclusive of the other. In fact, managers become better when they have good leadership skills. Leaders are better when they have good management skills. Both leaders and managers are of critical importance to any vital and thriving organization, whether it is a two-person partnership or a multinational corporation.

Leaders are not often found in *routine* managerial positions. If talented leaders are placed in a managerial role, they are likely to quickly elevate those roles to ones of higher importance and influence. If not, they typically move on to a role that better enables them to use their talents. Their behavior will be dominated by leadership skills more than management skills. They may still fulfill management functions, but more of their energy will be channeled into leading.

Sometimes, leaders fulfill practically no management functions. For example, a gifted scientist working to discover drugs that are effective against cancer may not perform any management functions at all. But the scientist clearly is leading. A software engineer who develops new technologies may also perform no management duties, but the engineer is definitely leading others.

However, leaders who are responsible for groups or organizations but do no managing must at a minimum *oversee* an effective management function delegated through other people for their organization to be successful. If not, they are negligent in leading effectively.

Why Is Focus upon Specific Leadership Behaviors Important?

To become better at anything requires more than visualizing the end result and then having the sufficient desire to accomplish it. These are both absolutely necessary. But it is much less likely the end will be achieved without the disciplined focus upon the correct actions necessary to achieve the goal. The ability to learn a technical skill such as programming or a more abstract skill such as marketing is a product of understanding the actual steps that enable the necessary skill or requirement at hand.

> *If talented leaders are placed in a managerial role, they are likely to quickly elevate those roles to ones of higher importance and influence.*

Daniel is Michelle's supervisor in the customer service department; if he tells her she needs to "become a better communicator" and leaves it at that, she may likely be confused about what she is supposed to do. In fact, if that's all Daniel tells her, a case could be made that Daniel needs to become a better communicator himself. And in fact, one of the most common criticisms of people in group contexts is that they need to communicate better. Yet too often there is very little definition or direction on just exactly what that means.

Ambiguous orders rarely result in satisfactory outcomes. Without a complete understanding of what someone else is talking about, complete communication has not occurred. On the other hand, if Daniel had told Michelle she needs to listen more carefully to customer requests and ensure understanding of their issue before filing a service request, she would be in a better position to improve her communications skills.

Leaders and managers are often held more accountable for ensuring adequate communication than others in teams and organizations. Providing specific direction on expected outcomes and behaviors that support effective communications at all levels is vital for success in the domain of leadership. The scope of leadership includes so many interactive variables, including person-to-person communications, that without a clear understanding of what is required for the situation at hand, there are likely to be problems.

This does not mean that leaders have to go into great detail every time they delegate or issue a directive. It does mean that they must ensure that others understand specifically *what* is to be done. If they determine that the other party needs more detail, then they supply just enough to ensure understanding of what they mean.

What Is the Most Common Behavior that Leaders Need to Improve?

The highest priority behavioral needs of leaders are a function of at least three variables. The first is their existing strengths and limitations. The second is the special demands and requirements of their span of leadership and the role they play. The third is the talents or deficiencies of their team. An accurate and objective assessment of each of those variables will determine the behavior that is most in need of improvement for that particular leader. And those variables range significantly across endless leadership contexts.

Regardless, the most common area of work performed by leadership coaches as well as management seminars has to do with communications skills. And within that realm, the skills that usually receive the most attention have to do with listening. The need to strengthen this behavior is generally inclusive of almost all leadership roles, whether in business, sports, the military, education, or anywhere two or more people must work together.

Ironically, when supervisors and managers who rate their associates or supervisors low on communications skills are rated by their team members, they are also often rated low on the same scales themselves. Obviously, few people recognize poor communications skills in themselves, even though they can detect them in others.

Why Are Communications Behaviors so Critical for Leaders?

Relationships between people are, at their most basic level, simply an exchange of information, and the quality of that exchange determines the quality of the relationship. The exchange may be verbal, physical, or visual. It can even be the result of an action (or inaction). But in all cases, the exchange of information communicates a message. It is the *message* that influences others. If poorly constructed, the person delivering the message loses credibility (or, even worse, may have a negative impact upon others). If well constructed, the message will build credibility and can lead to a positive outcome. Because of this fact, the most important variable in the influence and power that leaders exercise is through their communications behaviors.

Messages leaders communicate through their behaviors can be liking or disliking, interest or disinterest, caring or indifference, respect or disrespect, teaching or suppressing learning, and so on. The message may address how, why, when, where, or any of an unlimited number of other variables. But ultimately, at the core of it all, is an exchange of information that will either establish or erode the leader's influence and promote or undermine positive results.

What Can Leaders Do to Strengthen Their Direct Communications Behaviors?

The three most natural vehicles for the exchange of information with others are auditory, visual, and kinesthetic. The dominance of each modality is determined early in life. By the age of six, most children unconsciously choose one of these modalities as the manner through which learning best occurs for them.[38] As a result, some people are much more influenced by what they see than what they hear. Others are more attuned to what they hear than what they see. And some learn best by doing rather than watching how something is done.

> *The most common area of work performed by leadership coaches as well as management seminars has to do with communications skills.*

Cross modalities among people can become a significant challenge in the process of day-to-day communications between individuals in the work setting. Determining which vehicle is the primary method for someone is a significant advantage for any leader in building relationships and fostering improved communications.

Leaders can begin to determine which method is most important by observing how a person reacts to each of the three vehicles. The person's response, the questions they ask, and their actions that indicate the impact of the message are a few considerations that identify which vehicle has the most impact. Importantly, leaders should never assume that their own preferred method of communication is the same as anyone else's.

What Is the Influence of Technology on Interactive Communications?

Today, the overreliance on technology, such as text messaging, emails, and social media, sometimes deters the *kind* of communications that are necessary to promote complete understanding between leaders and others. Communications expert and author Kathy Condone[39] discusses the challenge of counterbalancing the growing reliance on technologies for communicating with others. While she promotes the practical value of popular social media as well as text messaging and emails to keep others abreast of one's activities, she cautions against overdoing it.

Social media, text messaging, emails, and related tools are convenient and have great utility for updating others on one's activities. But when it comes to resolving sensitive issues between people, face-to-face communications cannot be replaced by texting and emails. Often, such modes of communication that are used to replace face-to-face communications can actually heighten the challenge of resolving sensitive issues between people.

Attempting to handle sensitive issues or complex human relations through technological modes of communication often makes the problem worse by precluding the most essential element of human communication: direct contact, person to person. The lack of direct in-person interaction, which provides the opportunity to read nonverbal cues such as facial expression and tone of voice, dramatically limits significant components of the communication process.

It is essential for effective leaders to encourage direct and genuine communication wherever and whenever practical. And that begins with the leader, as he or she sets the standard for what is most acceptable within his or her scope of influence.

What Role Does Nonverbal Communication Play in How a Leader Communicates?

In addition to the content of the words expressed, the powerful effect of nonverbal communication has been highlighted by many research projects and scholarly publications. For example, Professor Albert Mehrabian has been a leading pioneer in understanding nonverbal communications since the 1960s. According to Mehrabian's research, widely accepted by many in the field:

- 7 percent of messages pertaining to feelings and attitudes is in the words that are spoken.
- 38 percent of messages pertaining to feelings and attitudes is paralinguistic, such as the way that the words are said.
- 55 percent of messages pertaining to feelings and attitudes is in facial expression and the stance of the speaker.

Mehrabian posits that emotions and attitudes establish the domain of communication that focuses upon relationships, roles, and interactive requirements between people.[40] His research indicates that effective communications skills are largely functions of information that people, and especially leaders, express unconsciously. Even the way people walk and move can communicate their attitude or feelings, without them being aware of the messages they are sending. Because leaders are often more visible than others, keeping this fact in mind is paramount to their ability to influence others positively.

A consideration that can be especially valuable for leaders managing communications between themselves and others has to do with two basic streams of information between people. One is content, and the other, process. Content is what people communicate.

> *When it comes to resolving sensitive issues between people, face-to-face communications cannot be replaced by texting and emails.*

It embodies the conceptual, such as an idea or the description of an event. Process is how people behave. It embodies the actions that demonstrate what a person is about at a particular moment. If a leader's content and process are not congruent, all manner of problems may arise, including being accused of hypocrisy and insincerity. And communications between leaders and others are always occurring on both paths simultaneously. This requires that leaders be especially mindful of ensuring their integrity. This is because what they say and what they do will likely receive much more scrutiny than anyone else in their sphere of associates.

What Other Behaviors Are High Priorities for Ensuring Effective Leadership?

The nature of the leadership role determines which behaviors are priorities for any particular leader. For example, the decision making behaviors of value for the leader of a product development team may include promoting the sharing of ideas before choosing a course to pursue and collaborating to allow everyone on the team to challenge existing paradigms. But the decision making behaviors most appropriate for leading in an emergency, such as fighting a fire, may be making quick choices among several options, the adherence to established procedures for the type of emergency situation, and deferring answers to the whys and wherefores of choices of action. In each case, the marked difference in appropriate behaviors is a function of the circumstance.

The variety of behaviors that are important within most leadership contexts beyond communications are then established by the specific situation. The LBI exercise at the end of chapter 4 lists some of the most common important behaviors for leadership positions involving teams. Behaviors listed on the LBI that are normally high priorities within team settings are included within the categories of decision making, confidence, foresight, courage, and trust. However, other categories may be higher priorities in another setting, contingent upon the specific needs of the team, the situation, and the abilities of the leader.

What Face-to-Face Behaviors Strengthen a Leader's Ability to Engage Others?

As referenced earlier, everyone has unique variables that affect the quality and depth of their direct interactions with others. Personality style, roles, and values; the effects of auditory, visual, or kinesthetic messages; and many other variables are part of the equation. It would be impractical for new leaders to ascertain what level of information they need when meeting team members for the first time.

As a result, leaders must often identify behaviors that quickly promote a legitimate dynamic between themselves and others. There is no absolute formula that provides the most utility in all cases, but there is at least one critical behavior demonstrated by effective leaders that almost always encourages effective communications: being genuine. While that may sound simple, it is not always easily accomplished.

There numerous conventions leaders must overcome in demonstrating genuine communications behavior with others. Sometimes, those conventions are a function of stereotypical roles people assume about leaders and how they should behave toward them. Sometimes, it is a function of assumptions leaders themselves make toward others. Additionally, many of the daily person-to-person interactions people have are brief, such as passing in a hall or meeting others hurriedly. Those kinds of interchanges can challenge even the most effective communicators.

An example is illustrated by the common convention of asking "How are you?" when meeting someone. That particular exchange, as well as others such as "Have a nice day," has become so automatic that it is rendered practically meaningless. And in fact, such exchanges can lend themselves to insincere, robotic speech: that which is automatic and unthinking. While it is understandable how such a convention can become commonplace in a fast-paced and complex societal context, it often only serves to undermine genuine communications in all contexts.

> *One critical behavior demonstrated by effective leaders that almost always encourages effective communications is being genuine.*

It is not uncommon to greet someone with, "It's good to see you John," and receive a robotic response such as "Fine. How are you?"

indicating that John did not listen to your greeting to begin with; he is simply responding without thinking. There are simple steps to counteract such shallow dynamics. A sincere "Hello Alyssa, it's nice to meet you" in a first encounter, instead of "How are you?" is more likely to indicate you actually are pleased to meet someone. Or while passing a coworker in a hall, smiling directly at them and stating, "Good morning, Kevin," typically goes much further than the automatic "How are you?" that is so often completely hollow.

To become highly effective at promoting genuine communications, leaders must learn how to overcome such conventions. And it is the leader's responsibility to set the precedent for genuine communications that will eventually dominate the culture of their team or organization.

How Are Effective Leadership Behaviors Best Learned?

From the day we are born, we begin a process of learning that lasts throughout life. When learning ceases, our quality of life deteriorates rapidly. While there are many ways to define learning, it always entails a relatively permanent change in behavior as a result of knowledge and experience. Learning anything requires acquiring new perspectives and behaviors, as well as reshaping *existing* perspectives and behaviors. A person who continues to evolve and acquire new knowledge, concepts, perspectives, and behaviors continues to be vital. A person who does not, loses vitality.

As referenced in chapter 3, thinking patterns, which include attitude, perspective, biases, and other processes, are often deeply engrained habits and behaviors. Changing deeply conditioned human behavior is not easy.

Because learning goes on at a variety of levels, each level plays a part in the development of the total person. The various levels of learning in becoming a more effective leader occur not only at the conscious level but at the subconscious level as well. Additionally, learning occurs at the physical level, such as the communications expressed by nonverbal body language or tone of voice.

Various theories of learning provide important perspectives as to how human beings best acquire sophisticated behaviors, such as leadership, and what transpires during the learning process.[41] Cognitive theory provides significant insight on what occurs in learning to become an effective leader. Cognition is the mental action or process of acquiring knowledge and understanding through thought, experience, and the senses. It involves such functions as perception, sensation, intuition, and various mental processes that affect all facets of learning.

Human beings can learn efficiently by observation, taking

> *When learning ceases, our quality of life deteriorates rapidly.*

instruction, and practicing effective behavior they observe in others, based upon their cognition. As a result, many of the more sophisticated behaviors we acquire, such as leadership behavior, may be facilitated by emulating what we perceive as performed successfully by others. Newly acquired behaviors don't just occur because we understand a better way to do something and then automatically imitate or adopt the new behavior. We must actually work at it through conscious effort and practice. This all begins at the cognitive level.

What Important Considerations Does Cognitive Theory Reveal that Facilitate Improved Learning of Leadership Behaviors?

During cognitive learning, individuals begin the learning process by observation, listening, reading, or experiencing, and then they *process and remember* the information. But additionally, they must have a vehicle to apply what has been learned to ensure that it becomes a natural behavior occurring automatically or with little conscious effort.

In some cases, cognitive learning at a conceptual level might seem to be passive learning, because there is often no motor movement involved. However, the learner is active, in a cognitive way, in processing and remembering new information. Additionally, recent research studies prove that heart rate, respiration, and even chemical processes within the central cortex change during learning whether motor movement is involved or not. Experiments on the glucose level in the blood before, during, and after challenging mental activity show that glucose levels are drained with such mental effort.

However, at the cognitive level of learning, even when learning is approached in the most objective manner, it is often subject to biases of which the learner may not even be aware. As discussed in chapter 3, the research of Dr. Daniel Kahneman, summarized in *Thinking Fast and Slow,* suggests that cognitive biases have a powerful influence upon one's perspective and interpretation of events and consequently how they learn. From assessing choices to substitution of opinion for fact, Kahneman's research suggests that people, even good leaders, often place too much confidence in their judgment over gathering well-grounded facts before making decisions.

Furthermore, Kahneman's research underscores the need for leaders to focus upon learning *valid* behaviors that yield results as opposed to making ungrounded assumptions of what might work in leadership contexts. Because any new behavior must displace existing patterns of behavior, which are often highly influenced by biases and ungrounded judgments, the focus must be on behaviors that prove effective.

Beyond learning new behaviors, cognitive learning contexts also enable one to create and transmit sophisticated information and knowledge that includes values, beliefs, and norms. This is critical to principle-based leadership, which is based upon respected values and norms of behavior.

In What Ways Does How a Person Think Affect Their Leadership Behavior?

How people think shapes what they think. How people think influences the way they *interpret* information and experience which will shape their thoughts and perspective. This then highly influences what they think. Consequently, what people think guides their choices, decisions, reactions, and behaviors, which largely shape their personality and regular behavior pattern.

How people think is a deeply conditioned behavior. It is a function of experience, formal and informal education, and the influence of others. It may be demonstrated by the degree of open- or closed-mindedness; the inclination to look for potentially positive (or potentially negative) outcomes in events; being resistant to change or intrigued by its potential; tending to be more influenced by emotions than facts; forming quick opinions versus forming carefully considered opinions; and so on. How we think then ultimately establishes the paths by which we process and act upon our daily experiences and the information we receive. Because of this fact, *leaders must be especially alert to how they think* and the affect it has upon their relationships with others as well as their own ability to be successful.

Dr. Daniel Amen, a distinguished fellow of the American Psychiatric Association and founder and medical director of the nationwide Amen Clinics, is a highly respected authority on the functioning of the human brain. He is well known for his work on the tie between brain physiology and mental processes. Dr. Amen's research and his clinical work on mental health have made contributions to the fields of human dynamics and relationship skills that are especially important for leaders.

Because leaders in direct contact contexts must not only be effective with relationship skills but also gain the confidence of others in their ability to lead, the insights provided by Dr. Amen's research are particularly valuable in shedding light upon how *habits of thinking* can work for or against people in leadership positions.

Amen suggests that our overall mind state has a certain tone or flavor based largely on the types of thoughts we think.[42] It is deeply conditioned and automatic. *In Change Your Brain: Change Your Life,* he emphasizes the value of learning to look at one's own thought patterns objectively to determine the ultimate influence they may have upon success, whether for good or bad:

> *Unfortunately, there is no formal place where we are taught to think much about our thoughts or to challenge the notions that go through our head, even though our thoughts are always with us. Most people do not understand how important thoughts are, and leave the development of thought patterns to random chance. Unless you think about your thoughts, they are automatic or "they just happen." Since they just happen, they are not necessarily correct. Your thoughts do not always tell the truth. Sometimes they even lie to you . . . . Positive thoughts and a positive attitude will help you radiate a sense of well-being, making it easier for others to connect with you. Positive thoughts will also help you be more effective in your life . . . . What goes on in your mind all day long can determine whether your behavior is self-defeating or self-promoting.*

Dr. Amen goes on to propose that you can train your thoughts to be positive and optimistic, or you can allow them to be negative and work against the self as well as others. This point is especially important to people in leadership positions because of the critical need for them to exercise a positive influence within their span of authority.

A more positive outlook tends to evoke more confidence in a leader. It also serves to increase the leader's mental state, which can enhance creativity, relationship skills, rational decision making, and every other important mental process required to be an effective leader. This may in turn serve to promote more positive paradigms within and about the leader as well as establish a foundation of respect for the leader's character.

Leaders who are guided by positive paradigms may be more likely to focus upon promoting and demonstrating service-oriented behavior, because they tend to look for what is right with others versus what is wrong with them. They focus more upon possibilities and hopes. This is how they think. As illustrated from the interview of William R. Alvin in chapter 2, such considerations as convenience, political influences, or self gain are less important to principle-based leaders, if important at all. The "how" part of their thinking by and large influences "what" they think and is often manifested in seeking ways to serve others above their self-serving interests.

However, because every leader is an individual and possesses specific characteristics, even if they are guided by principles, how they think will be unique and can't be absolutely typecast. But what differentiates the way

> *You can train your thoughts to be positive and optimistic, or you can allow them to be negative and work against the self as well as others.*

principle-based leaders think are principles that guide them toward outcomes that others are more likely to find admirable. And this fact generally holds true, even during periods of great challenge or change.

What Behaviors Support Leaders' Management of Change?

Change is not unique to any age or period. It is common throughout history. However, we hear more about it today because new technologies, global economic factors, and cultural norms are evolving so rapidly. And that affects change. So while change is a constant, the rate and scope seem to be ever increasing. Many people feel that things ought to stay the same; they are uncomfortable with this constant fact of life. Successful leaders don't succumb to this kind of thinking and, in fact, often drive change, as it enables them to shape the direction it takes.

Effective leaders, as a natural requirement of their role, must be forward thinking; they therefore continually keep sight of changes that can occur. To be a successful leader, it is not enough to simply be aware that change is always possible; leaders must be ready to react and know what to do to capitalize on change. They continually work to manage it successfully.

Change may be categorized in two general forms: purposeful and necessary. Sometimes (but not always), the need for change is based on both forms simultaneously. In purposeful change, leaders act as change agents. They *purposefully decide* that there is value to be captured by change. The change is not for the sake of change but for the sake of improving results. Necessary change on the other hand is required to *sustain viability*. It is necessary when a team is not meeting its goals. And in fact, if it does not change, the team, group, or organization may fail.

It's important to note that sometimes change is undertaken inappropriately, simply for the sake of change, because it *sounds good*. The reason may be to appear progressive, to increase already successful results even more, or any of a number of other ill-conceived purposes. More likely than not, that kind of change is a mistake.

> *Never change a winning game; always change a losing one.*—Bill Tilden

This lesson was ignored in the 1980s when the Coca Cola Company introduced its New Coke product. The decision turned out to be a marketing fiasco. New Coke was developed to replace the original formula; it was conceived to increase market share, even though Coca Cola had been the market leader since its inception ninety-nine years earlier.

> *Effective leaders, as a natural requirement of their role, must be forward thinking.*

New Coke originally had no separate name of its own; when it was introduced in 1985 it was simply known as "the new taste of Coca-Cola." In 1990, it was renamed Coca Cola II, but public reaction to the unnecessary change was negative. The new product turned out to be a monumental failure, resulting in loss of market share. When the original formula was rebranded as "Coca Cola Classic," the soft drink regained its lead in market share.

Often, companies, organizations, and even politicians will trumpet the word "change" without even describing what the change will entail, hoping to gain support. In fact, the public is often fooled into believing that the change will be for the better. Far too often, this is not the case.

In the early 1930s, prior to Adolf Hitler becoming chancellor of Germany, he gained support by promising "change" as well as unity and peace if the people would follow his plans for National Socialism. He described these plans in his book, *Mein Kampf* (*My Struggle*). Unfortunately, few German people actually read that book or looked closely into the political methods he used to gain power. If they had they would have learned about his distorted views that would ultimately bring rampant destruction and misery to his country as a result of his failed conquests. But before that disastrous outcome and because of Germany's economic woes, the political differences dividing the county, and the uncertainty of the times, "change" sounded good, regardless of what it might bring. As history recorded, the change Hitler wrought was an unmitigated disaster.

Regardless of whether change is a function of purpose for the right reasons, or simply necessary for survival, leaders must manage either type of change with the same behaviors. And these behaviors are of value almost without regard to the size or scope of the leader's organization. Effective leaders must demonstrate some or all of the following behaviors in managing successful change:

1. Prediction. This anticipatory behavior focuses a leader's attention on the *most likely outcomes* of variable activities for the team or organization.
2. Critical thinking. Strategic perspective concerning long-term trends and potential results to identify possible outcomes. It requires understanding the *forces* that will shape the future.
3. Preparation for change. Because change is inevitable, the only question is how much time will pass until it occurs; the effective leader ensures that the organization has the *resources* in place to adjust and prosper as change occurs.
4. Innovative thinking. *Leaders spur innovative thinking* by modeling it, encouraging it, and rewarding it. In respect to change, these innovations address the elements that define the nature of the change affecting the organization.
5. Understand *what is changing and what is not changing*. This behavior is subjective and is a function of the leader seeing through the maze of multiple considerations to identify those that embody the actual state of affairs.
6. Stay abreast of change as it occurs. Consider other options and alternatives that surface as change evolves and *uncover hidden possible opportunities and threats*.

Each of the aforementioned behaviors has been successfully applied throughout history by strong leaders regardless of the change addressed or the impact upon groups, cultures, or even nations. Change is a given. And the methods for managing change, though boosted by technological advances and techniques, are still essentially the same as they have always been.

How Does a Leader Identify the Most Critical Behaviors They Should Develop?

As referenced earlier, the most pressing needs for developing specific leadership behaviors vary from leader to leader.[43] Completing the LBI is often a good first step to determine which of your behaviors need the most attention. It may also be worthwhile for others who know you to complete the assessment as well. Those persons must be credible and be willing to evaluate you objectively, discuss your strengths and weaknesses candidly, and evaluate you constructively. Their feedback should include specific instances that illustrate your performance, and you should take their feedback with an open mind.

Valuable assessments, whether the LBI, validated assessment instruments, or other exercises, to have the most utility must avoid generalizations and stay focused on specific behaviors. This is best achieved by mentioning explicit instances that can be observed.

For example, if a leadership coach suggests that a client needs to think like a visionary to increase innovation in his or her organization, this advice may merely raise the point for consideration and promote other questions, such as, "What can I do as a visionary to spur innovation?" Unless the behavior is observable or can be measured, the "what to do" is missing. "Thinking like a visionary" is not observable. However, the products of thinking like a visionary, once they are transferred to action, are observable.

Some actions involved in thinking like a visionary may include organizing and facilitating strategy sessions, encouraging individual team members to submit written recommendations, and bringing in experts to discuss the latest creativity tools in line with developments in the company's markets.

Finally, leaders must identify their most important behavioral development needs by ensuring objective and balanced assessment through informed and valid sources that focus upon the specifics of "what to do" to improve their effectiveness. The focus on behavior, whether for self-improvement or other skills that involve interacting with others, is an essential part of the equation.

Chapter 5 Summary

- It is only what a leader *does* that makes the difference between success and failure for themselves and others.
- Leadership is exercised less through words and more through *observable* behaviors and activities that affect what the leader wants to accomplish.
- Relationships between people are, at their most basic level, a process of an *exchange* of information.
- *Listening* skills are an absolute requirement for effective leadership and are often the most critical developmental issue in leadership roles.
- *Nonverbal* communications usually have much greater impact on others than spoken words.
- *How* a person thinks, shapes *what* they think.
- *Change is inevitable,* and effective leaders must always be ready to adjust to and manage change in the best interest of their teams and organizations.

Assessment Exercise #4

Chapter 6 will examine differences between leadership activities and managerial activities and the interdependence between the two. You will obtain much more value from the chapter by completing a self-rating on your own managerial behavior (if such an exercise applies to your role). Go to the GreenbrierLeadership. com homepage, click on the blue "Additional Assessments" tab, and then select the box titled "Managerial Behavior Index" (MBI). You can print out the assessment. After completing it, save the results for application in chapter 10.

CHAPTER 6

MANAGERIAL SKILLS

The leader of any organization is ultimately responsible for ensuring a competent managerial function. Leaders may perform managerial tasks themselves or delegate them. But without an effective management function, the organization will not survive, and the leadership will have failed. While in some respects, the management function might seem less glamorous than the leadership function, the two are inextricably bound in organizations that prosper.[44] As referenced in chapter 5, while there are differences between leadership and management functions, the two must support each other.

Whether it's the leader or a manager within the leader's scope of authority, a strong managerial function must continually evolve if the organization is to thrive and succeed. The managerial function includes the responsibility for capital as well as human, technological, and intellectual resources and administrative activities of the organization. And as previously emphasized, good managers must possess good leadership skills.

While leadership has more of a focus upon human processes and management has more of a focus on resource allocation,

> *Whether it's the leader or a manager within the leader's scope of authority, a strong managerial function must continually evolve if the organization is to thrive and succeed.*

they must both be well coordinated to ensure success. The following section compares leadership and management functions and behaviors.

The Manager Implements; the Leader Originates

The manager's job is to apply *existing* policies and procedures to ensure that the organization's activities and functions are fulfilled as designed. The manager may or may not have been responsible for establishing the policies and procedures. Regardless of who established them, ensuring adherence to them is a management function.

The originality the leader brings to the equation has to do with identification of new ways of doing things. Leaders should not be bound by convention; instead, they should continually seek better ways to do things. Obviously if the leader were bound by strict adherence to the status quo, there would be no real progress.

The greatest advances in science, technology, culture, and economics always come from original thinking that transcends existing ways of doing things. Once the new idea is originated, taking it from the conceptual stage to the practical stage is more often than not accomplished by people with excellent management skills who know how to implement the ideas.

The Manager Administers; the Leader Innovates

Administration is the broad and varied process of running an organization. It entails all of the activities in place to carry out its functions. It normally follows a pre-established framework of how things are done to fulfill operations. Administration focuses upon implementation of plans within the existing structure of people involved in its use. It promotes consistency and predictability.

Innovation spurred by leaders does not ignore existing administrative processes; it is often *contingent* upon them. Innovation does not discard existing systems; it identifies better ways of doing them. For example, an innovation in wireless communication technologies does not preclude the concept of wireless technology. The innovation still is a wireless technology, but it may be done in an improved and possibly more cost-effective manner.

> The greatest advances in science, technology, culture, and economics always come from original thinking that transcends existing ways of doing things.

Innovation, which is a leadership function, differs from invention in that innovation refers to the use of a better, more original idea or method, whereas invention, also a leadership function, refers more directly to the creation of a totally new idea or method.

The Manager Copes with Reality; the Leader Investigates It

Managers often attempt to operate in a world of "givens." Their job is to do the best with what they are unable to change. That is not to say they shouldn't seek to make changes, but regardless of whether they are successful in that endeavor or not, they must work with existing resources and circumstances to sustain the functions for which they are responsible.

As a result, managers are more *inclined* to operate within prevailing circumstances before they invest effort in the investigative process. In some cases, this means operating within challenging circumstances. It is up to the manager to ensure smooth and successful functioning of the organization, regardless of what may occur.

Investigations undertaken during the leadership function seek to understand what is happening, with the goal of learning from or altering it. Leaders investigate circumstances with the goal in mind of resolving or capitalizing upon a situation. Managers, on the other hand, are more likely to work within the existing circumstance, unless they are forced to investigate an issue that is affecting operations.

The Manager Maintains; the Leader Develops

Maintaining is the sustaining of operations in a smooth and consistent fashion. It requires the manager to pay careful attention to each facet of the machinery that makes up all of the operations of the organization. The manager may do this alone or with others, depending upon the size and scope of the organization. This function usually requires daily attention in any organization, regardless of size.

Strong leaders develop organizations as well as people. Because leadership is about finding or creating new paths, it continually seeks to promote progress. Effective leaders exercise significant influence through the progress of the people they manage and encourage. However, such progress can only be sustained through the effective management of people and processes.

The Manager Focuses on Systems and Structure; the Leader Focuses on People

Good managers do care about the welfare of people in the organization. They have to, because in order to get anything done, they must work effectively with others. However, their primary focus is typically on *results* in respect to goals, standards, and objectives. They are responsible for working within existing systems and structures that define what gets done; their world is often dominated by performance measurements and standards.

Sometimes, managers must put people's feelings and desires second, after bottom line results.[45] This is not to say they should not place a high priority upon people's needs. It means that managers often have to defer attention to those requirements until after addressing the organization's operational requirements first.

Because managers' successes are contingent upon the efforts of other people, they have a decided advantage when they possess strong leadership skills and instincts. Strong leadership abilities enable them to best capitalize on the full capabilities of others in their organization and achieve their goals.

The Manager Relies on Control; the Leader Promotes Trust

Because managers are normally held more accountable for following existing policies and procedures and achieving measurable results, they might believe they have less flexibility in straying from established methods of doing things. This may or may not be the case, depending upon the organization. Nevertheless, managers are more about controlling resources, including *human* resources, than leaders. The manager's formal authority therefore is often more relied upon for such control than the ability to inspire others toward high performance.

Leaders, on the other hand, are more about influencing people to go above and beyond the basic requirements of their job, including following defined performance standards. They inspire initiative. Leaders work to boost performance and the contributions of others as a function of appealing to more intrinsic rewards.[46]

In order for leaders to accomplish this, others must have deep trust in their values, integrity, and character. If they do, they are much more inclined to develop the kind of respect for the leader, which will promote their involvement beyond mere obedience. This enables the leader to inspire greater contributions from others in areas of creativity and initiative than basic compliance typically yields.

The Manager Has a Near-Term Perspective; the Leader Has a Long-Range View

How far out managers and leaders view things is a function of what they are attempting to accomplish. Typically, the management function has more to do with *sustainability* of existing operations and systems. Consequently, managers are often responsible for controlling costs, monitoring current circumstances, ensuring day-to-day compliance with operating procedures, and other functions focused on the near term. This is not to say that managers

> *Effective leaders exercise exponential influence through the progress of the people they manage and encourage.*

don't have to keep sight of the future; they do. But they are frequently more focused upon the here and now.

Leaders, in order to ensure continuing success and vitality, often pay attention to far reaching trends that may affect their organization. Because they *are* leaders, they tend to be alert to potential signs of opportunity or things that may change in the future. To do this effectively, they have to be mindful of what the past has taught them, what the present affords them, and what the future may offer them. This requires a strategic orientation that looks beyond the scope of controlling current circumstances and making the most efficient use of existing resources.

The Manager Asks How and When; the Leader Asks What and Why

Because managers are often principally accountable for the here and now, they must by the nature of their role be more bound to specific current guidelines. Managers often have a pressing challenge: to figure out how to best use existing resources, handle existing circumstances, or solve present-day problems. In addition they must know when things have to be done to keep operations on track.

Leaders are often more interested in the *what* and the *why,* because they are interested in uncovering solutions that might enable them to invoke productive change or identify new paths toward success. Good managers with strong leadership skills may do the same thing, but oftentimes they have to make immediate results a priority. Therefore, they may not be afforded the flexibility to look more closely into the "what and why" side of the equation.

The Manager Does Things Right; the Leader Does the Right Thing

Managers are very much about making sure there is compliance with existing procedures, standards, and rules. They often establish these rules and then are responsible for enforcing them. As managers, they are responsible for ensuring that things run the way they are supposed to. The *right* way.

Leaders, of course, also want things to be done the right way. But because they often focus more attention on the values, culture, and spirit of the organization, they must make sure that team members *feel* positive about the direction of the organization. And this means they must always keep sight of doing what is recognized and accepted as right in principle to increase the likelihood of gaining the commitment of their team.

This point bears emphasis, because it is sometimes misunderstood by those in leadership positions. What is right is not always what employees or team members want; it is not always what is popular. The leader doing right is often a product of well-grounded principles that may transcend what others want. It is based on what the leader knows is in the interests of the greater good for the entire organization, though it may be unpopular. However, most people intrinsically know what is right and usually respect a leader who pursues that course in spite of resistance.

The management role is ultimately responsible for *carrying out* the specific activities and goals defined by the leadership of the organization. But the leadership is responsible for ensuring that the activities of the management function are *congruent* with the organizational direction and goals, stemming from the top.

Obviously, if the person in the top leadership position is also the manager responsible for carrying out management responsibilities, the implementation should be smooth. If the implementation isn't smooth, it's likely the leader is not managing effectively, or there may be a breakdown of communications or incompetence at the staff level between the leader and the individual functional managers.

For example, David is the general manager of a manufacturing firm in a corporate structure that includes five plants. He is responsible for ensuring the complete profit and loss as well as product selection, with a minimum of direction from the executives in the corporate office. In essence, he is in the top leadership position for that plant. The functional managers (such as engineering, the controller, distribution, operations, and human resources) report to David's office.

If there is a problem in implementing the long-term strategy established by David, it is squarely his responsibility to correct it. He will have to do so by taking actions that either redirect or replace those people who are not fulfilling their duties as established specifically by him. In that David is directly vested with the responsibility for

> *The manager does things right; the leader does the right thing.*

both leadership and management of the plant, he must function in both roles simultaneously. He can't delegate the responsibility for correcting problems to anyone else. He may have his staff work with him in solving the issues, but as both leader and manager, he must be at the center of the solution. This is one of the most difficult roles in all organizations.

There is no end to the number of behaviors that support effective management by leaders, whether they delegate them or direct them personally. The following list highlights some important *management functions* leaders must ensure are fulfilled in mid to large sized organizations:

> ## *Organization and Planning*

Managers must establish and communicate goals and priorities for themselves and others. This is performed not only for day-to-day activities, but also for longer term goals: quarterly and annually. Often this requires breaking projects or tasks into specific activities with time frames to track results. And because almost nothing ever goes exactly as planned, effective managers must often handle crises or unexpected demands expediently, in a manner that does not suspend or undermine operations.

> ## *Supervision*

The supervisory function is the direct link between management and employees or team members. It can be one of the most stress inducing roles in any organization because the supervisor is often held directly accountable for results or lack of results of their team members. Additionally supervisors must deal directly with performance problems, and emotional issues of employees, and are held directly accountable for much of what occurs in the work setting.

Managers, at the least, oversee the supervisory function, if they do not provide it themselves. It is the supervisor's responsibility to provide clear direction to team members to ensure they understand what duties are to be performed. The supervisor must consider the knowledge and skill level of team members when assigning work and assist in monitoring performance as necessary and appropriate to ensure success.

➤ *Development of Others*

Managers are responsible for the selection, hiring, training, and long-term development of everyone in the organization. Effective development focuses upon identifying the specific learning needs of team members and offering appropriate training as required. An important part of the development of individuals is providing regular communication with them in respect to their performance as well as their developmental needs. Effective performance appraisals are not delivered once a year or by using a preprinted form. They are part of an *ongoing and regular open communication* process; this may or may not involve an annual evaluation form. Planned reviews simply support the process.

➤ *Decision Making*

Sound decision making is a product of applying logic and critical thinking to analyze problems or options adequately before making a decision.[47] When there is not sufficient time to deliberate, good managers are able to make quick and objective decisions under stress as necessary. Additionally, considering others' perspectives when possible is an indication of collaborative decision making, which is an asset in effective management.

➤ *Time Management*

An organization's management is responsible for ensuring that scheduled goals, actions, and tasks are performed in respect to formally established deadlines. The same requirement is true of how managers perform their own individual responsibilities. In order to accomplish this, managers must regularly set aside time to work on high priority tasks when less likely to be interrupted as well as apply other effective time management techniques as practical. To make the most effective use of an organization's resources, managers should continuously look for ways to do things more efficiently.

> ## *Interpersonal*

Good managers are good with people. They are able to work well with a broad variety of personalities and cultural backgrounds, at all levels. Understanding the various motivational needs of team members and considering them while supervising is an essential skill. In order to accomplish this, managers have to build genuine relationships and rapport with team members. This is a product of behaving with others in a manner that indicates respect and concern for their welfare.

> ## *Conceptual Skills*

In order to promote effective operations of any organization, managers must be able to analyze complex situations and develop operational strategies. This requires coordinating a broad variety of activities and varied interests to ensure results. Managers must view the organization in totality and understand the interdependence of all parts under their span of responsibility.

> ## *Technical*

To guide and direct the activities under their authority, managers must have sufficient knowledge of their organization's processes to provide competent direction. They do not have to know more than everyone within their span of authority, but they have to know enough about operations to oversee them in a competent manner. They definitely must demonstrate excellent proficiency in their own essential responsibilities. The ability to acquire sophisticated skills necessary to oversee application of processes is a necessity if they are to perform in a competent manner, build respect for their value, and oversee the efforts of others.

➢ *Communications*

Managers get things done through people. There is no more important skill required of a manager than to communicate effectively. This includes promoting and fostering open, two-way communication at all levels. Demonstrating excellent listening skills by response and follow-through action gives managers a distinct advantage in gaining cooperation at every level. Providing clear and concise messages, orally and written, that others readily understand is necessary to manage them effectively. And similar to outstanding leaders, the kind of language managers use should demonstrate professionalism and promote dignity toward everyone with whom they interact.

> *Sound decision making is a product of applying logic and critical thinking to analyze problems or options adequately before making a decision.*

➢ *Delegation*

Whether managers supervise directly or indirectly through their staff, delegation is the primary tool that establishes what is to be performed and by whom. The ability to delegate in a supportive manner while avoiding micromanagement enables managers to attain more value from others.* If delegated tasks do not go smoothly, managers should avoid overly critical feedback to continue to earn respect as well as promote better performance. Before the task is begun, managers should determine who will be responsible for following through to ensure completion as planned.

> *[You may go to Greenbrier Leadership.com and click on the blue "Additional Assessments" tab; select "Delegations Skills Assessment" to take a self-assessment exercise on delegation skills behaviors. The exercise will enable you to identify

and prioritize activities to improve your delegation skills in practical settings.]

> ### Problem Solving

The problem-solving ability of managers greatly influences the level of authority and responsibility they ultimately carry. People who are effective problem solvers tend to rise quickly. No organization, small or large, is without problems. To be successful in this endeavor, managers must frame problems clearly and completely before attempting to solve them. That typically requires working closely with others to identify viable options and develop practical solutions that can be attempted within a reasonable time frame. Collaborative skills typically foster good problem-solving efforts.

> ### Resource Management

This is the management function that is centrally responsible for maximizing the most return and utility from all existing resources. This includes capital resources, material resources, human resources, and everything else within the organization. Managers are responsible for considering cost and quality issues in respect to all organizational activities. Additionally, managers should promote an environment that is conscious of responsible use of resources at every level, even those not directly within their authority.

In summary, while the leadership role *guides* the organization, the management role *marshals* the substance of the organization. Management coordinates *all* of the organization's resources. That includes the entire sphere of operations. Without competent management of financial, human, and technical resources, an organization cannot succeed.

Chapter 6 Summary

- The leader of any organization is ultimately responsible for ensuring a *competent* managerial function.
- The management function entails *all* decisions for what will be done in the organization and how it will be accomplished.
- Managers and leaders *knowing* what to do "right" is a product of applying principles that transcend what others want or what appears most expedient.
- The managerial function includes full *responsibility* for the capital, human resource, technological, intellectual, and administrative activity of the organization.
- While the leadership role *guides* the organization, the management role marshals the *substance* of the organization.
- Without competent *management* of financial, human, and technical resources, organizations cannot survive.
- Excellent managers must also have *leadership* skills to be successful, as everything they do either impacts others or requires their involvement.

CHAPTER 7

ASSESSMENT OF TEAM MEMBERS

Exceptional leaders constantly promote the best in themselves and others. They do this whether they are in a formal leadership position or simply interacting with others. *Excellence* is a standard that defines most of what they do. In respect to promoting the best in others, leaders with formal responsibility must know how to assess the capabilities as well as the liabilities of others in order to lead them effectively. Additionally, they must be alert to the most significant variables that affect each team member's performance.

The challenge of understanding how to enable the best in people varies depending upon each individual. Everyone is unique, and astute leaders know not to make general assumptions about what affects the performance of any individual. They know that to truly understand a person's capabilities, it's necessary to assess them objectively and appropriately, relative to the role they play. All people are subject to a variety of considerations that affect how they behave and what will encourage them to perform up to their potential.[48]

There are many dimensions that work in concert to affect how people behave: personality, ability, skills, incentives, emotional makeup, knowledge, personal circumstances, as well as a variety of other considerations.[49] From a practical standpoint, leaders cannot know about each of those dimensions for any one person, let alone a group of workers.

> *Everyone is unique, and astute leaders know not to make general assumptions about what affects the performance of any individual.*

However, effective leaders quickly learn enough about team members in order to promote their performance.

As illustrated in chapter 4, people have very different behavioral styles, roles, and values that affect how they behave. But in addition to those considerations, leaders need to understand much more about the *capabilities* of their team members to help them succeed. Even well-trained professionals in the field of assessment, such as psychologists, psychiatrists, and counselors, never know everything about why people behave the way they do or what goes on in their minds. The human psyche is affected by complex considerations, many of them quite obscure.

However, there are some universal considerations affecting most team members that leaders can assess in order to improve their performance. But it takes time to fully determine what drives any particular person's performance. In fact, assessment of an individual never stops, because what affects their behavior almost always changes. Sometimes, that is a product of what is going on in the work setting, and sometimes, it is a function of what is occurring in their lives outside work.

The following list indicates some common universal dimensions that leaders can use to better understand others and encourage good performance in teams or work settings.

➢ Knowledge
➢ Skills
➢ Abilities
➢ Interactive style
➢ Role expectations

➢ Values
➢ Incentives
➢ Relationship requirements
➢ Developmental needs

These particular dimensions can be categorized into three distinct groups. Category A contains knowledge, skills, and abilities. Category B consists of interactive style, role expectations, and values. And Category C addresses incentives, relationship requirements, and developmental needs.

The actual order in which such dimensions should be prioritized for assessment can vary significantly among individuals.[50] However, as leaders gain a reasonable understanding of each of these dimensions for each individual, they will be in a much better position to accomplish the most important thing a leader can do for others: promote and enable constructive and rewarding use of a person's talents to achieve important ends for themselves as well as others.

Though the order in which these assessments may or ought to be performed for any individual can vary, normally there is a preferred sequence for them.

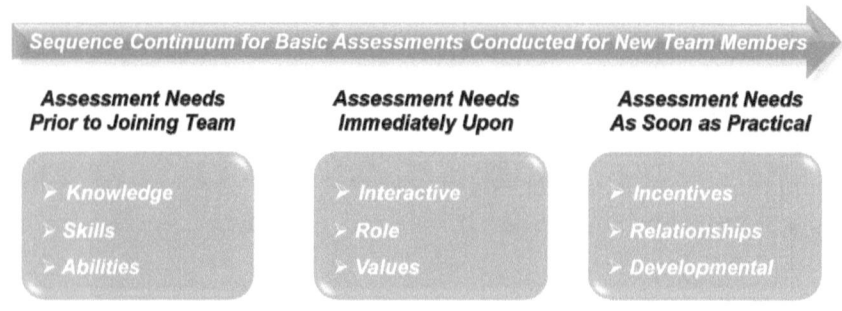

Sequence Continuum for Basic Assessments Conducted for New Team Members

Assessment Needs Prior to Joining Team	Assessment Needs Immediately Upon	Assessment Needs As Soon as Practical
➤ Knowledge ➤ Skills ➤ Abilities	➤ Interactive ➤ Role ➤ Values	➤ Incentives ➤ Relationships ➤ Developmental

Category A. Knowledge, Skills, and Abilities

Category A, knowledge, skills, and abilities (KSA), should be assessed *prior* to hiring someone or assigning them to a new position. KSAs are often used to establish selection criteria for filling positions in public sector as well as private employment settings. However, defining them can be valuable for almost any position.

The KSAs are the specific requirements employers establish when filling a particular position. They may be used to compare candidates and rank their suitability to open positions. The ability of a job candidate to meet the KSAs will establish their suitability to fill the position. This will in turn determine whether they receive serious consideration.

Knowledge

This dimension is the summation of all cognitive learning that is retained and available for recall and application. Obviously, it includes everything acquired through formal education, informal education, and experience; this information is acquired from reading, watching, and study as well as every other source of learning. Some learning experts even maintain that intuitive and unconscious information can also influence a person's behavior.[51] Regardless, for our purposes, everything a person knows that is valid and has value qualifies as practical knowledge.

In respect to a job applicant's suitability for a specific position, the knowledge dimension may be described as an *organized body of information*, often factual or procedural in nature. For example, having knowledge of human resources rules and regulations could be used as a KSA for a position as a human resources specialist. To demonstrate such knowledge in a job interview, candidates should be able to describe their job-related knowledge. They should also be able to make the case specifically in respect to how such knowledge was applied in their past jobs and the value of that application to the specific duties and responsibilities of the position for which they are applying.

> *Everything a person knows that is valid and has value qualifies as practical knowledge.*

Astute managers and leaders are adept at quickly determining how the unique knowledge of any particular person may translate to value for their team or organization. This enables them to identify the best ways to leverage the individual's knowledge in order to benefit both the individual and the team.

Some people possess more knowledge than is first apparent. It is the leader's job to encourage them to access that knowledge for constructive purposes that benefit the person as well as others. Of course, a leader is not going to be able to do that without first building enough rapport to determine what lies below the surface of the individual.

Skills

The specific skills people possess are what determine their value in their role or job. That should be the primary reason they were hired. However, sometimes there is not a good fit of skill to the position, and it's not discovered soon enough. This can be very costly in many ways.[52] Not just financially but also in respect to a broad array of capital and even emotional costs for a number of people including the new hire.

Wise leaders and managers will ascertain as best they can the actual skill value of team members *before* they join the organization. Often, during the early going in a new job or role, the person's true skill level may not be determined. It may take a while to gain an accurate assessment of their capabilities once they are in the position. Even if leaders do not supervise the person directly, they are still responsible for ensuring, as early as practical, that their level of competence is appropriate for the role.

Generally, skills refer to a person's capability to perform activities and duties that encompass a particular job. This includes the capacity to apply that ability to perform whatever tasks are necessary. For example, people need computer skills if they are to work with computers regularly. There are currently available many outstanding validated testing instruments that enable managers to assess a candidate's skills.[53]

Even more than knowledge, people's skill level is at the core of their value to a team or organization. Without the ability to perform competently, they have little value in their assigned role, regardless of their level of knowledge.

The world cares very little about what a man or woman knows; it is what a man or woman is able to do that counts.—Booker T. Washington

As mentioned, sometimes a team member's actual proficiency and skill is very difficult for a leader to assess quickly. That can occur if the skill is specialized and the leader lacks the background in this particular area of expertise. It may also be difficult to assess because it takes time to measure the results of their performance. Regardless, the *skill level* people apply to their role is often the most critical dimension leaders must assess about those within their span of influence.

> *Even more than knowledge, people's skill level is at the core of their value to a team or organization.*

Abilities

Ability is the capacity to perform an activity or task; for example, a medical lab technician needs the ability to use instruments to analyze blood samples. The level of ability ties specifically to the role the person fulfills in the organization. However, ability may also refer to the totality of what an individual is capable of. It can include natural abilities not yet fully developed.

Some valuable abilities are sometimes hidden. Individuals may not even be aware of their abilities if they have never used them. It's not unusual to discover outstanding talents in artistic, athletic, or academic areas as people become exposed to new activities. In fact, some latent abilities are never tapped because people don't have the opportunity to use them or have no awareness of them.

As leaders learn more about people's abilities directly related to their role, as well as the potential they have beyond their role, they can encourage them better. This is the responsibility of a good leader or manager. This kind of assessment is a function of leaders knowing more about an individual than can be determined by routine interaction or day-to-day observation. It requires leaders to build a meaningful relationship or at least gain sufficient information about a person's capabilities that go beyond the basic facets of their role. It is also a function of having systems in place to evaluate, encourage, and train team members to improve their performance.

Category B. Interactive Style, Role Expectations, and Values

As soon as practical after new team members assume their role, they should be assessed according to Category B: interactive style, role expectations, and values. Chapter 4 described these dimensions, which involve the interactive dynamic that naturally occurs among people. Beyond a team member's actual skills and potential utility, these are the dimensions that make each person unique. They are in large part a determinant of personality; they differentiate team members even more than their skills, knowledge, and abilities.

While they are not often formally assessed in employment interviews, these dimensions may nonetheless have a great impact upon the interviewer. In fact, if a candidate builds a rapport based on common values and develops a good interactive dynamic with the interviewer, this often carries more weight than job-related qualifications.

Interactive Style

As discussed previously, style can refer to a leadership approach or *how* people conduct themselves in various roles; it is the distinctive manner in which people behave. It focuses upon how a person interacts with others, communicates, carries out work, and generally relates to others. Additionally, style addresses non-interactive behaviors such as how much detail they demonstrate on tasks, how they manage their time, and other deeply conditioned habits. Knowing the *interactive style* of team members is of great value to leaders as they work to build mutual respect.

As leaders assess the interactive style requirements of team members, it's not necessary to administer a formal assessment exercise (although that can be very valuable). However, leaders must pay attention to how team members communicate and perform their work. For example, if one person appears to need detailed explanations, leaders should pay attention to that requirement and provide the depth of information necessary. If other team members like to communicate in an open and friendly manner, then leaders should consider that as they flex their style accordingly.

Perhaps most importantly, and when practical, leaders will be in the best position to assess the interactive needs and abilities of team members by *learning to listen carefully*. Not just listening to the content of the spoken words, but focusing on the deeper meaning of what is being communicated. By genuinely seeking to understand what others are communicating, and how they communicate, leaders gain more understanding of what is being expressed. They can promote rapport and mutual respect by working to accommodate each individual's communication requirements.

Role Expectations

Chapter 4 described role expectations from the perspective of the individual. Other individual team members' perspectives on their role may or may not be consistent with how they see themselves. However, it is important that leaders understand what role individuals on their team *think* they play within the larger framework. This provides more understanding of team members than just identifying the role they are formally assigned. Leaders must understand the responsibilities people assume, as well as the activities they undertake, to influence them constructively.

Leaders can only assess this variable accurately by developing enough of a working relationship with individuals to observe what they do, how they do it, and what they perceive as their challenges. Whether a systematic performance appraisal or evaluation process is in place or not, such a dialogue should still occur. No formal appraisal process can replace the value of ongoing natural rapport and communication.

Values

Values include not only what drives people's level of effort but also what satisfies them. People's values are immensely important to them. The values people embrace are a function of at least two separate influences: natural interests and the influence of their life experience.

What is important to people is not necessarily predictable from their background or education. In part, people's values may be influenced by personal preferences as part of their genetic makeup. Additionally, the role and influence of experience has a powerful impact upon values. Childhood influences, cultural norms, life-altering events, and many other factors affect what people establish as important.[54]

Similar to determining incentives, leaders must build enough of a mutually respectful relationship with team members to learn how their values influence their behavior. This is often achieved by talking with individuals about their interests. Good leaders build enough genuine rapport with team members for them to recognize that the leader takes a genuine interest in their wants and needs, within the work setting and in general.

Category C. Incentives, Relationship Requirements, and Developmental Needs

Soon after new team members assume their role their manager may evaluate them according to Category C: incentives, relationship requirements, and developmental needs. Managers and supervisors often do not learn quickly enough about these dimensions of their team members. However, they should try to learn about them as soon as practical.

This category might have the most influence upon factors that can motivate people working in groups. This section discusses the potential rewards that influence effort, the dynamics that affect how people feel about the organization, and the tools that lay the groundwork for success. Astute managers who demonstrate good leadership skills will pay careful attention to these considerations for all their team members.

> *Leaders will be in the best position to assess the interactive needs and abilities of team members by simply learning to listen carefully.*

To determine the effect leaders have on the job satisfaction and commitment of their direct reports, Zenger Folkman, an organizational consulting firm in Orem, Utah, gathered data from nearly 100,000 respondents in hundreds of different organizations. Direct reports rated the effectiveness of their immediate manager and the level of satisfaction and commitment each had with the organization. After examining numerous factors that influence employee satisfaction and commitment, one consideration was consistently shown to have the most impact on performance and success: the *leadership effectiveness* of the employees' immediate manager.[55]

> *The quickest and most reliable way of increasing employee satisfaction and commitment is to provide employees with a more effective leader.*—Joseph Folkman

In part, and more often than not in large part, the level of motivation and success of team members is greatly influenced by their leader or manager. Part of this has to do with knowing how to appeal to specific incentives that motivate employees. But in a more important way, having a manager with outstanding leadership skills may, by their sheer force of personal influence,

> *The quickest and most reliable way of increasing employee satisfaction and commitment is to provide employees with a more effective leader.*

outweigh pay, recognition, security, and other factors. Leaders with charisma combined with caring and genuine enthusiasm tend to foster much higher levels of performance. In fact, genuine enthusiasm is one of the most positively infectious emotions; it can be the most powerful tool to evoke the best in others.

Incentives

Incentives are the *potential rewards* that drive individuals toward any activity. For example, some people are motivated by the desire to make a significant contribution to their organization or team. Astute leaders will endeavor to learn which incentive appeals to each individual within their span of responsibility in order to better encourage their performance.[56]

Typically, there are many incentives that apply across a group of people, even in small organizations. The list below describes the "Five A's" exercise that can illustrate how individual incentives vary widely in respect to their priorities, even in the same organization. The five categories of rewards, which are usually available in most organizations, are used to establish priorities for individual team members. They include:

> ➢ Autonomy: the freedom to work with a relatively high degree of independence
> ➢ Achievement: the opportunity to work toward high goals
> ➢ Affiliation: feeling like an important and valued member of a group or team
> ➢ Affluence: to gain significant monetary reward based upon performance
> ➢ Authority: the degree of control that enables one to make significant contributions

While each of these incentives typically has some measure of value to most individuals, there usually will be varying degrees of interest from person to person. The leader may ask members to prioritize them from most to least important. Knowing how a person prioritizes these incentives, or any other potential incentives, will help the leader understand more about what influences their performance.

The five incentives described here are limited, considering there are often many others of significance, but the idea is to illustrate the importance of how people *prioritize* some common potential rewards. Because people's priorities are often not static, leaders should stay close enough to team members to know what is important as time passes. As leaders learn how individuals prioritize incentives, they gain a little more insight in understanding what motivates them.

For example, the pie chart illustrates the priorities of Alison, a member of a project team at an IT services provider. Alison places the highest priority on the opportunity to work alone or at least with a high degree of autonomy. But because her project team must work closely as well as collaborate regularly upon their goals and products, autonomy is for the most part unavailable to her. However, because achievement is also very important to Alison, the opportunity to gain it as a result of good performance is likely to be an important incentive to her. If her team leader recognizes this fact the leader will be well advised to identify ways Alison may attain a high level of achievement by working effectively with her team members as well as performing well.

Alison's Priorities on the 'Five A's' Exercise

- 1 *Autonomy*
- 2 *Achievement*
- 3 *Affiliation*
- 4 *Affluence*
- 5 *Authority*

Of course, as in Alison's case leaders may often not be able to deliver the most important priority for every individual. As in the example above, if the individual would like more autonomy, but it simply isn't available because of the nature of their job, a leader can't do anything about that. However, by knowing what other priorities are important for that person, and the priorities other team members place upon each potential reward, the leader is better informed to encourage improved performance for the team as a whole. This approach can be an important factor in affecting not only improved performance of a team but more job satisfaction for each individual.

Relationship Requirements

Even in small organizations, individuals often have very different work relationship requirements. Some people are much more comfortable working in a collaborative environment. Others prefer to work alone. The kinds of work relationships people are most comfortable with can be a combination of a variety of factors. Their interactive style, the level of competence of their teammates, the need for encouragement, and a broad variety of considerations can affect the kind of working relationships they prefer.

But regardless of specific differences among people in respect to their preferences for working relationships, one fact stands out. It is simply that people who become members of a group must relate to others if they are to play an important role in the success of the group. And leaders are impacted by this fact more than anyone. In part, leaders need to build relationships with individuals and encourage relationships among team members. To accomplish this, leaders will be more effective if they understand the individual relationship preferences and inclinations of group members.

In addition to those mentioned above, other examples of relationship needs of individuals in groups include how much contact and guidance they require on the job and how much performance coaching they may need. The level of rapport each prefers with team members is another example of an important relationship requirement.

Sometimes, the role a person wants to assume is especially important, even when it is outside the duties of their job. This may include the level of interaction the organization promotes beyond pure work-related processes or the opportunity to assist others with their work. Generally, relationship opportunities and requirements are products of the nature and culture of the work environment and how members relate to one another beyond the pure focus of their jobs.

Developmental Needs

If not discovered quickly, developmental needs (sometimes termed "deficiencies") can lead to serious problems for team members and the team as a whole. It is best to uncover such needs at the earliest point practical to promote growth.

Whenever new members of a team arrive, they deserve careful attention to help them fit in and to promote their competence in the new role. Such an orientation period is a critical variable that can affect the success of the new team members.[57] Leaders who ignore this important step may soon discover problems that could have been easily headed off with proper attention in the early going.

However, developmental needs do not just include deficiencies or immediate learning requirements. They also include those considerations that enable people to continue to grow in their position for the long run. They may be addressed through training at various stages, individual coaching, or regular opportunities to participate in learning-based programs that increase competence. Organizations that place a high priority on training, performance appraisal, coaching, and other professional development methods typically receive rewards that far outweigh the costs.[58]

Putting It All Together

While we have examined nine assessment dimensions important to leaders in direct contact contexts with team members, this is by no means a comprehensive list. Many other dimensions can help assess the capabilities and needs of team members, depending upon the specific context. However, the dimensions referenced should give you a good idea of the types of considerations leaders should address whenever feasible.

A good leader does not necessarily need to take a structured or highly systematic approach to assessing all of these dimensions; if possible, of course, that is recommended in order to learn enough about others to lead them effectively. If not practical to evaluate people in detail, effective leaders and managers still need to assess team members in a manner that provides enough knowledge to deliver optimal leadership and developmental support.

Assessing the capabilities of team members is essential to helping them improve; it will also give their contributions more value. This is why many successful organizations engage countless industrial psychologists, management experts, and consultants: to help increase the leadership abilities of their executives and managers and better develop employees at all levels.

While a number of factors may affect people's behavior and performance, understanding how to influence them positively is not complicated. It is a function of something successful leaders *can* control: their own behavior. As leaders build mutual respect, demonstrate admirable principles, communicate genuinely, and demonstrate competence in their role, their ability to influence others expands exponentially.

Understanding what motivates others is often a function of looking beyond what appears on the surface. But it does not necessarily have to be complicated or require a Ph.D. in psychology. It can be as simple as just listening carefully to what others say. This may sound elementary, but in fact the art of listening and understanding is usually a function entailing much more than hearing the words. It is often a product of insight. Such insight is frequently a function of developing a genuine interest and understanding what others are trying to communicate not only with their words but their actions.

For example, the great educator, author, and orator Booker T. Washington, who founded Tuskegee Institute, was a master at assessing his allies and his opponents without any of today's sophisticated assessment tools. He was the dominant leader in the Black American community from 1890 to 1915. In order to demonstrate his outstanding leadership on behalf of his constituents, Washington had to yield enormous influence against overwhelming odds.

One of the principle tools by which Washington accomplished his great achievements was his uncanny ability to recognize what others wanted and how they thought. His ability to assess people was in part intuition as well as looking beyond their words, basing his assessments more so upon their actions. He knew that actions speak louder than words.

His opponents called his powerful network of supporters the "Tuskegee Machine" and often mustered much opposition to his causes.[59] However, Washington was effective because of his ability to garner the support of numerous groups, including influential whites, black business owners, educational institutions, and religious organizations.

In order to gain support for his causes, Washington built strong relationships and developed mutual respect across a broad variety of arenas, including wealthy benefactors, politicians, religious leaders, and the public at large. He knew how to assess their values, needs, motives, and inclinations, regardless of their words. He *understood* people.

In summary, the ability to assess others, whether systematically or informally, is an absolute requirement for successful leaders. Leaders become successful through their influence over others, and that is largely determined by their ability to understand their capabilities, desires, and intentions.

Chapter 7 Summary

- Outstanding leaders *continuously* promote the best in themselves and others.
- Everyone is *unique,* and good leaders know better than to make assumptions about anyone without sufficient knowledge.
- Effective leaders learn how to identify and assess *relevant* capabilities of each team member to ensure the most value for the team as well as each individual.
- *Knowledge* is the sum total of everything we learn that we are able to draw upon and use practically or conceptually.
- *Skills* refer to the know-how and capability to perform activities and duties that encompass a particular job.
- Abilities encompass all of the obvious as well as hidden *capabilities* that each individual possesses.
- Many outstanding assessment tools and resources are readily available for managers to apply when practical to better understand the capabilities of their team.
- As leaders build mutual respect, demonstrate ethical principles, and communicate genuinely, their ability to *influence* others expands exponentially.

CHAPTER 8

LEADERSHIP OPPORTUNITIES

Leadership roles are best assumed naturally. That is, when leaders assume leadership roles as a result of accepting responsibility or through a spirit of service they are in the most opportune position to have value and exercise influence. This as opposed to assuming leadership roles as a function of seeking authority, power, prestige, or personal gain affords the leader more likelihood of building genuine commitment of followers. Some of the most well known and admired leaders in history rose to positions of leadership because they were in the right position, were right for the opportunity, or were willing to accept responsibility in the interest of serving others.

Because principle-based leaders embody a spirit of service they often find themselves in positions where they demonstrate leadership, whether they set out to do so or not. And sometimes, people not originally envisioned as having leadership potential learn that they are capable of outstanding leadership when the opportunity occurs.

As a child, Harry Truman wore thick glasses to compensate for poor eyesight. Smaller than other children his age and more interested in playing the piano and reading about history than playing outside

> *Leadership roles are best assumed naturally.*

with other boys, he became a loner. His close relationship with his mother led many people to consider him a "mama's boy." But Harry had a bold dream.

From elementary school through high school, Harry felt a strong sense of patriotism and a sincere desire to serve his country. As a result he set a personal goal of attending West Point.[60] But though he was an industrious and diligent teen as well as an excellent student, he was turned down by the military academy and then the Army because of his poor eyesight. This setback would have disheartened many young men his age and caused them to give up the dream of serving their country.

But instead, in 1905, young Harry applied to the Missouri National Guard. Again his poor eyesight posed a barrier. Undaunted, he returned a second time and had no problem passing the physical, as he had obtained a copy of the eye chart and memorized it.

After joining the National Guard, Harry worked his way up and eventually became an officer. By the time the United States became involved in World War I, Harry was a battery commander in the 129th Field Artillery regiment and was assigned to France. It was then that he received his first significant opportunity to demonstrate his leadership ability, which would become a hallmark in American history.

During a surprise bombardment by German artillery, many in his regiment panicked and began to flee their positions. While trying to rally his troops from horseback, Harry's frightened mount reared up and then toppled over on him, almost crushing him. Squirming out from under the horse, he stood up in the midst of shells exploding all around and continued to urge his men to return to their positions. The sight of their small but courageous commander, undeterred by the deafening thunder and flying debris of the explosions, rallied his men. They returned to their positions and held on until their mission was completed.

Truman wrote about that significant event in a diary he kept faithfully all during his service.[61] He wrote that he learned a couple of things about himself at that critical moment in his life. The crisis revealed that he possessed more courage than he had previously been aware. The other lesson was that he liked the challenge of a position of leadership. As with many who become famous leaders, he was pressed into a crisis situation and then was willing to assume responsibility in the face of great risk. Years later as president, in the closing months of World War II, what Truman learned that day enabled him to lead admirably and courageously, handling some of the most difficult decisions ever made by a wartime leader.

Are Some People Naturally Gifted for Leadership?

There are people who are unquestionably gifted to lead. Because of their personality, charisma or ability to organize others, they naturally assume positions of leadership, regardless of where they are. And they may overcome many obstacles along the way.

But regardless of what group they are members of, natural leaders are looked to for direction. Often they have a distinct sense of presence that stems from confidence and purpose. They may have a strong overt personality style, but this is not always necessary. More importantly, they have the ability to articulate goals and direction. And they can express clearly what must happen to reach those goals.

Leadership roles may be assumed by shouldering responsibility for organizing and exercising authority, or they may be a function of initiating new ideas in organizations, culturally, or technologically.[62] Invariably, persons with such abilities are quickly recognized as having great value that can benefit others. Such persons do not need to seek power or authority; it finds them because of their natural gifts.

> *Regardless of what group they are members of natural leaders are looked to for direction.*

Benjamin Franklin rose from meager beginnings. One of thirteen siblings, he had little access to formal education.[63] But he went on to become a founding father of the newly formed country that continues to revere him more than two hundred years later.

Franklin demonstrated many unusual leadership abilities. He began leading early as a successful businessman with his printing company. He became one of the most well known authors of his day. He went on to serve as the first postmaster general of the United States. Additionally, Franklin was a highly respected political theorist and politician. He founded many civic organizations, including a fire department and a university.[64]

Most notably, Franklin played a central role in the creation of the United States, through his persistent and unflagging campaign for unity among the original thirteen colonies. When he became ambassador to France, he embodied the image of a statesman from an emerging nation and was instrumental in garnering French support during the American Revolution. Many cite this feat as critical to the Continental army defeating British forces and ensuring independence.

Franklin's leadership abilities were even demonstrated technologically; he made many discoveries related to the properties and physics of electricity. His inventions include the lightning rod, bifocals, the Franklin stove, and an odometer. He was a musician and invented the glass harmonica. He was a popular satirist, a leading statesman, and a civic activist. Through speaking, writing, and involvement with other leaders of the American Revolution, Franklin became a chief architect of the emerging nation.

Franklin embodied the value of service through community activism and civic contributions. He promoted the Puritan values of truth and moral characteristics as hallmarks of good and responsible citizenship. The values of hard work and thrift were consistent themes in his writings.

In essence, Franklin modeled principle-based leadership in every facet of his long and fruitful life. Because of his principles and his abilities, he would have been a great leader no matter where he found himself. Regardless of situation, circumstance, or barriers to success, people like Benjamin Franklin often assume positions of leadership. But in reality, people with such natural gifts are very rare.

What Common Barriers Must Leaders Overcome to Assume Leadership Roles?

Everyone has hurdles in life that could undermine their success and happiness. People can be distracted from using their intellect or talent by health-related issues, a lack of educational opportunity, negative childhood experiences, financial instability, or countless life circumstances. That is a common fact of life from which no one escapes. However, there are far too many incidences of people who overcame seemingly impossible obstacles to become great leaders to allow anyone the excuse that they were held back by circumstances out of their control. The lesson is that anyone can rise above their circumstances. Despite overwhelming obstacles, the following people achieved great success:

- Abraham Lincoln had what was then called melancholy (now termed depression).
- Winston Churchill had bipolar disorder.
- Ludwig von Beethoven was deaf.
- William Wilberforce, an abolitionist in Great Britain, suffered from ulcerative colitis, which in those days was treated with opium. This treatment was severely detrimental to his health, and he was slowly poisoned.
- George Hale, who led a fourteen-year project that created the Mount Palomar telescope (twice the size of any other telescope in the world at that time), had schizophrenia.
- Helen Keller became one of the greatest advocates for people with disabilities, women's suffrage, and other social causes, despite being blind and deaf.
- Nick Vujicic was born with no arms or legs. Shunned in childhood by other children, he went on to found the Citipointe Church in Brisbane, Australia, and become one of the most in demand motivational speakers in the world.
- Albert Einstein had dyslexia.

People with outstanding leadership qualities are irrepressible. Their persistent nature is a central characteristic in their makeup. Because of that fact, whether they face health issues, oppressive circumstances, discrimination, economic disadvantages, or any of a number of misfortunes, they prevail. In addition, such leaders typically demonstrate a selfless focus that spurs them on to serve others naturally.

Who is an example of an unlikely great historical leader?

A world famous pioneer humanitarian Clara Barton overcame enormous obstacles to become an icon of public service that benefited millions.[65] After founding the American Red Cross, Barton became one of the most well known and respected leaders in the history of nonprofit public service. But her beginnings did not indicate much promise. In fact, up through her twenty-eighth year, she was unknown.

Barton did not become a leader simply by being in the right place at the right time. She rose to leadership positions because of her irrepressible spirit and ability to gain respect demonstrating value in a variety of circumstances. In fact, she experienced many setbacks that could have stifled her outstanding achievements had she not possessed unrelenting persistence.

In 1850, when Barton was twenty-nine, she enrolled in the Clinton Liberal Institute in New York to study writing and language arts. After completing her study, she managed to secure financial support to initiate a free school in New Jersey, offering education in writing and language arts. The school's enrollment soon grew to over 600 students. The school's size then required hiring a board of directors as well as a full-time headmaster. Ironically, although Clara had founded and built the school, the board ignored her interest in becoming the headmaster and hired a man instead. Such discrimination in respect to professional roles against women was common at that time.

In 1855, Barton decided to move to Washington DC to pursue a position in the US Patent Office. She became the first woman clerk hired by the US government. She was also paid the same as men working at a similar level, which was unheard of during this time. Unfortunately, under pressure and political opposition toward women working in the government, her position was soon downgraded to copyist. And shortly after that, her position was eliminated altogether.

However, Barton persisted. She continued to seek reemployment at the Patent Office and was rehired in 1861, shortly after the election of President Abraham Lincoln. She was successful in this role, as her male counterparts

> *There are far too many incidences of people who overcame seemingly impossible obstacles to become outstanding leaders to allow anyone the excuse that they were held back by circumstances out of their control.*

recognized her outstanding value and innate leadership. However, shortly after assuming this role, her father became gravely ill. She journeyed to his home, as he was not likely to live much longer.

Before her father died, he convinced her that it was her duty as a Christian to somehow provide assistance to soldiers in the Civil War. In April, following his death, Barton returned to Washington with an idea of how to provide direct aid to soldiers.[66] She began to gather medical supplies, bandages, food, and clothing to distribute on the field of battle. She wanted to care for wounded soldiers on the front lines but was denied this opportunity because it was not considered acceptable for a woman to be exposed to battle conditions. However, undaunted, she persisted, and in August of 1862, she was given permission to work on the front lines.

Eventually, Barton gained support from many influential people who supported her mission of mercy on the battlefield. In 1864, she was appointed as the "Lady in Charge" of the hospitals at the front by Union General Benjamin Butler. She endured many harrowing experiences, including an incident in which a bullet tore through the sleeve of her dress, striking and killing the man she was tending. She became known as the "Angel of the Battlefield." After the Civil

War ended, Barton went on to found the Red Cross, which has brought aid to millions worldwide.

How Important Is Authority to Exercise Influence as a Leader?

As referenced in chapter 1, influence is not a function of authority. Influence is a function of inducing commitment of others to follow because they *want* to. It is more driven by what others feel about the leader than their title or formal position. Influence is often established by the principles leaders represent rather than their formal role.

During the years Helen Keller was opening doors to opportunities for the blind, she had no formal authority. But she knew how to inspire and influence others to join her in worthwhile causes. Her courageous and unrelenting pursuit to lead a productive life of service, although blind and deaf, stirred admiration and support from almost everyone who learned about her. Her influence and the results she gained were momentous, even though she had practically no formal power or authority.

In 1906, at the age of twenty-five, Keller was scheduled to attend a meeting of the Association for Promoting the Interests of the Blind. However, she was unable to attend because of illness.[67] Up to that point, she had been instrumental in building the organization and was committed to seeing it prosper. Because of the tremendous respect she had garnered nationally, she was able to convince Samuel L. Clemons, better known as Mark Twain, and perhaps the most famous public speaker of the day, to take her place at the event.

> *Influence is a function of inducing commitment of others to follow because they want to.*

She wrote Clemons a letter that illustrates how great leaders may influence others with a message that touches hearts and can move mountains. On the day of the event, Clemons read her powerful letter aloud to all attendees; later, he even included it in his autobiography. The audience was stunned into silence by the passionate and powerful words in the interest of persons with disabilities. Shortly thereafter, public support for the organization was boosted exponentially.

Are Only Natural-Born Leaders best Suited for Leadership Roles?

The fact is that only a small percentage of people possess obvious natural leadership qualities. And then only a fraction of that group demonstrates the skills of Clara Barton, Benjamin Franklin, or Helen Keller. If only those kinds of persons actually assumed leadership positions, there could be no order. Anarchy would ensue, as not enough leaders would be available to govern or focus others toward mutually beneficial goals. But almost everyone has the potential to demonstrate leadership ability, depending upon the situation. There is a "leader within" just about everyone that will emerge if the person is willing to accept the responsibility. When people find themselves in situations that match their strengths, interests, and abilities, they know what to do and how to influence others. The critical variable is whether they care enough about others to assume responsibility.

Jaime Escalante was born in Oruro, Bolivia, in 1930. Before immigrating to the United States, he taught physics and mathematics in Bolivia. When Escalante first arrived in the United States, he worked odd jobs while teaching himself English. He eventually earned a college degree in California.[68]

In 1974, Escalante was hired as a teacher at Garfield High School in Los Angeles. However, the students attending his classes were so poorly prepared that he doubted they could fulfill the requirements of his class. He actually contacted his former employer in Bolivia about returning there to teach again. However, shortly before his planned departure, twelve students came forward and indicated interest in learning algebra from him. In that moment, because of those dozen eager students and his spirit of service, he decided to persist in his efforts at Garfield.

Shortly after his decision to stay at Garfield, the school's accreditation was threatened because of its students' poor test performance. The school system had a history of substituting compliance with the interests of political interests concerning class size, academic standards, and quotas in lieu of maintaining acceptable educational standards. He and other teachers were pressured to lower academic standards in the interest of keeping enrollments at minimum levels to receive federal and state monies.

Instead of succumbing to politicized goals that undermined academic standards, Escalante decided to press forward and offer advance placement calculus to his students. He was criticized by an administrator for requiring students to answer a homework question before allowing them into his classroom. When asked about the incident, Escalante said, "He told me to just get them inside, but I said there was no teaching, no learning going on."

> There is a "leader within" just about everyone that will emerge if the person is willing to accept the responsibility.

Determined to change the status quo at Garfield High School, Escalante convinced a few students that their futures would be much brighter with the right academic preparation. He persuaded them that a strong education in mathematics would open opportunities in engineering, electronics, and computers. He explained that careers in those areas would be in great demand in the future and command higher salaries than nonprofessional positions.

In the early going at Garfield, the school administrative heads opposed Escalante. He was even threatened with dismissal by an assistant principal because he came in too early, left too late, and failed to get permission to raise funds to pay for his students' advanced placement tests. And when demand for attendance in his classes began to rise, the teacher's union protested the number of students he allowed in his classes, as it exceeded the maximum number their labor contract mandated. However, in the face of such opposition, Escalante stood firm. He was far more interested in serving and delivering value for his students than comfort and a secure job.

Eventually, opposition against him decreased, as parents, students, other teachers, and finally administrators began to show respect for his leadership in the cause of excellence. Aside from allowing Escalante to continue his approach to teaching math, a new principal, Henry Gradillas, inspired by Escalante's example, overhauled the academic curriculum at Garfield. The principal required those taking basic math to take algebra. Following Escalante's lead, the principal also denied extracurricular activities to students who failed to maintain a C average and new students who failed basic skills tests. In 1978, Escalante taught his first calculus class. The school became renowned for the unusually high performance of its students on mathematics placement tests.

In time, Escalante's achievements became the subject of a book by Jay Mathews. In 1988, the book, *Escalante: The Best Teacher in America,* inspired an award-winning movie, *Stand and Deliver.* The movie detailed the path of Escalante's leadership and success in education. Escalante was soon receiving encouragement and visits from political leaders including then President Ronald Reagan.

Can Hidden Leadership Potential be developed by Simply Placing Someone in a Leadership Role?

It is possible. However, the potential repercussions of placing an unqualified individual in a position of leadership often far outweigh the possible gains. While most people have the potential to demonstrate leadership in some capacity, at least two prerequisites are needed to increase the likelihood of their success in a leadership role.

The first is that they are driven by a genuine desire to serve and work in the best interests of others, as opposed to taking the position for self-gain. Placing someone in a leadership role because they happen to be available, because they meet preconceived selection criteria or in order to advance their development negates this prerequisite.

The second prerequisite is that they have sufficient knowledge, skill, and ability to lead others. An effective leader must possess the appropriate knowledge to ascertain what needs to be done and how to work with others toward appropriate goals. Their abilities should include knowing how to promote mutual respect, make good decisions, solve problems, and other requirements pertaining to leading others. And in fact, that is how the best leaders normally assume leadership positions: Their knowledge and abilities persuade others to want them in a leadership role.

If people placed in leadership positions do not have the requisite knowledge, skills, and abilities, it is likely a great disservice to them as well as to others. And because it will be obvious to others that they have been placed in the role for inappropriate reasons, there is liable to be some resentment and resistance. No one can become a true and respected leader until others accept them as a leader; it is against human nature to force such an important dynamic arbitrarily.

Can Leaders be formed by Unexpected Crises?

Many people assume leadership positions because of circumstances that arise unexpectedly. They accept responsibility when unexpectedly called upon by the needs of others around them. These people rarely perceive their response to the emergency as extraordinary. They often continue to consider themselves as ordinary even after

The potential repercussions of placing an unqualified individual in a position of leadership often far outweigh the possible gains.

responding successfully to the crisis. But when the need became imminent, they demonstrated unusual ability as leaders.

It is often only during difficult challenges that we see the best in people. Challenges can evoke capabilities in the most dramatic ways. It's not especially difficult to look good or sound good when things are easy. Many people achieve positions of authority in political, social, or business organizations because of their image. But what is below the image they project on the surface may be quite different from their appearance or the words they used on their way to grasping power.

It is when problems and challenges arise that we learn about the true capabilities of others. In those moments, people with genuine leadership ability will understand what must happen. It's then that they rise to the occasion. They may not even think of themselves as a leader when they step up. They just know someone has to do something, and instead of looking around for someone else to respond, they look within themselves and do it.

There are countless such cases in history. Individuals often rise to serve as a leader at the moment of crisis and then fade back into their everyday routine when it is over. And some continue in leadership roles beyond the moment that propelled them to demonstrate their leadership ability. However, in all cases, these leaders were faced with a decision between two clear options. One was to avoid risk and pursue a safer route away from inconvenience, challenge, or potential harm. The other option was to step forward and be willing to serve others.

On the morning of September 11, 2001, Rick Rescorla, a security officer for Morgan Stanley's office in the World Trade Center, heard a terrific explosion.[69] He jumped up from his desk and stared out his window at an unbelievable sight: there was a huge hole high in the structure of Tower One, with clouds of ugly black smoke billowing out. The building had just been struck by a passenger aircraft. Just then, Rescorla heard a Port Authority announcement coming over the public address system. It urged everyone in his office to remain at their desks and wait for further instructions. Fortunately for the people in his area of responsibility, he ignored the order and took immediate action. Rescorla picked up his bullhorn and cell phone and began directing employees out of the building.

At one point, Rescorla directed people down a stairwell from the forty-fourth floor, continuing to calm them after the building lurched violently following the crash of the second plane, thirty-eight floors above. Morgan Stanley executive Bill McMahon later stated that hundreds of people taking a training class knew what to do because Rescorla led them to safe passage from the building. All during the crisis, Rescorla calmly led people down through the chaotic aftermath of the explosion above. Rescorla used his cell phone to get continual updates on news as he directed employees by bullhorn. He even managed to telephone his wife during the crisis to comfort her.

It is often only during difficult challenges that we see the best in people.

Because of his quick action in making a split-second decision to countermand an ill-conceived order from higher authorities, the employees he was responsible for made it safely out of the building. Rescorla methodically and coolly continued to guide hundreds of employees down the stairwell and outside. Once outside, they were directed by other officials away from the building to safety. Rescorla was last seen running back into the building to rescue more employees. But the building soon collapsed, and Rick Rescorla's remains were never recovered.

What Can a Person Do to Increase Their Opportunities to Serve in Leadership Roles?

Practically anyone with an interest in serving others is likely to find opportunities to lead eventually. Initially, they may only help or assist. But as they become more knowledgeable and valuable in their arena, they will have the opportunity to demonstrate initiative, pose solutions to problems, and suggest ideas. That kind of spirit is what fosters the best opportunities for learning how to lead.

Because principle-based leaders are interested in serving others, they are in an excellent position to establish mutual respect with them. Mutual respect is the foundation upon which all positive human dynamics are established. This is especially relevant in leadership roles. In essence, a person who leads in the context of service becomes a servant leader. That is the kind of leader that most people want to work with. And it is also the kind of leader that most likely will yield positive results for their followers.

As illustrated in many of the examples we have described, servant leadership is a philosophy as well as a set of principles and practices. Some believe that traditional leadership should focus primarily on the exercise of power by one at the top of an organization. That kind of leader is one that should be more focused upon wielding authority, with primary attention to achieving goals and results.

No leader is successful unless important goals and results are achieved. However, even beyond those objectives, a person at the top, if leading effectively, is still serving. This is because the servant leader uses authority only when appropriate. They put the needs of others first and help them perform as well as possible. Rather than function primarily in a directive capacity, they are able to balance enabling and supportive behaviors as necessary to better capitalize upon the abilities of the larger group.

The concept of servant leadership is ancient, with references to it going back before 500 BC. In China, passages in the *Tao Te Ching*[70] attributed to Lao-Tzu define it this way:

> *The highest type of ruler is one of whose existence the people are barely aware.*

Servant leadership can also be found in many religious texts, though the philosophy itself transcends any particular religious tradition. In the Christian tradition, the Gospel of Mark is frequently quoted in illustrating servant leadership:

> *Practically anyone with an interest in serving others is likely to find opportunities to lead eventually.*

> *But whoever desires to become great among you shall be your servant. And whoever of you desires to be first shall be slave of all. For even the Son of Man did not come to be served, but to serve, and to give His life a ransom for many.*—Mark 10:43-45

While servant leadership[71] is a timeless concept, it is believed by many that the phrase was coined by Robert Greenleaf in *The Servant as Leader*.

> *The servant-leader is servant first . . . . It begins with the natural feeling that one wants to serve, to serve first. Then conscious choice brings one to aspire to lead.*

Kent Keith, author of *The Case for Servant Leadership*,[72] states that servant leadership is ethical, practical, and meaningful. He identifies seven key practices of servant leaders: self-awareness, listening, changing the pyramid, developing your colleagues, coaching not controlling, unleashing the energy and intelligence of others, and foresight.

When taken together, all of the foregoing descriptions of the servant leader define someone who appeals to one of the most basic needs of the human psyche. That is that most humans are social beings who tend to want to function in a spirit of *togetherness and commonality*. This requires individuals to demonstrate a measure of selflessness to earn respect and be perceived as valuable to the group. This has the capacity to establish substantial meaning and purpose for many.

Chapter 8 Summary

- Leadership roles are best assumed *naturally*.
- People with outstanding leadership qualities are *irrepressible*.
- *Mutual respect* is the foundation upon which all positive human dynamics, including leadership roles, are established.
- The power to influence has much more to do with the *principles* or *causes* a leader represents than outward appearance or style.
- The critical variable for recognizing and assuming leadership opportunities is whether or not the person *cares* enough about others to assume responsibility.
- It is often only in difficult times that we see the *best* in people.
- Practically any person with an *interest* in serving others is likely to eventually find opportunities to lead.
- Principle-based leadership as a function of serving in the interests of others has been referenced in human history for millennia.

CHAPTER 9

CASE EXERCISES

Learning how to become better at leadership is best accomplished by *serving* in leadership positions. Real world learning from trial and error, including being open to counsel from mentors, peers, and persons within the leader's span of influence, as well as every other source of practical experience, is the optimal learning environment. However, obviously there is much value in being acquainted with conceptual issues related to leadership before, during, and after practical experience. This will facilitate accelerated leadership development.

In the last fifty years, there have been hundreds of books published that propose modern leadership techniques and philosophies. Many of them have outstanding value from a conceptual standpoint. Moreover, there are numerous excellent seminars and formal programs available as well as excellent schools of leadership. Many of these resources are valuable in preparing for and enhancing the leadership learning experience. Appendix B contains a list of a few popular books and programs available today.

But the gap between learning a concept and using a concept is often large. Many people who have a tremendous amount of conceptual knowledge, either because of a lack of opportunity or a lack of interest, do not apply it. As an interim step in taking information from concept to application, one learning tool that has excellent value is the case study approach. Case studies facilitate problem solving and encourage group discussion, providing valuable insights on how to use leadership concepts in real world situations. The case study has value not only in seminars but also in formal leadership development programs.

The following hypothetical cases illustrate some of the concepts included in this book. It's important to keep in mind that, similar to real life, there is not necessarily a single perfect solution or answer to the challenges presented in these cases. Rather than seeking the right answer, participants should *analyze and discuss* each case using concepts described in this and other works on leadership to identify reasonable options to address the issues.

The cases are better applied when two or more persons perform the analysis on an individual basis and then meet later to discuss the pros and cons of potential options. Readers who undertake to analyze the cases outside a team context should at the least discuss conclusions with another person who may provide another perspective. Each of the cases includes questions at the end. The questions are designed to promote review and application of the concepts covered in chapters 1 through 8. Potential responses to the questions are offered in Appendix C.

If you will be working on the case in a group setting, have each individual in the group read, analyze, and then answer the questions on their own. After that all members of the group should meet and compare notes in an open dialogue. All reasonable perspectives should be considered before agreeing upon an acceptable response to each question. The learning about leadership during such group discussion may greatly complement the content covered in the book.

The cases provided are brief. Obviously, in a real life circumstance, there would be many more facts and variables involved. But these short cases provide enough hypothetical substance that two or more people can discuss and debate options that might apply to similar leadership situations in real life.

Appendix C offers perspective on various considerations that may be of value after answering the questions for each case. However, the perspective provided in Appendix C is simply to remind you of some of the information covered in the previous chapters that may apply. Appendix C does not completely respond to each case, but it should remind you of material covered in chapters 1 through 8.

Case One. The Heir Apparent

After graduating with an MBA in marketing from an Ivy League school, David joined the small and successful West Coast manufacturer of aerospace instruments founded by his father. In the fifteen years since he joined the firm, David worked his way up to vice president of sales and marketing. In the last four years, David and three other vice presidents have been reporting to the founder, who was also the company's CEO. It was obvious to all in the organization, including the other three vice presidents, that David would take over the business when his father retired.

During his tenure as vice president of sales and marketing, David had done an outstanding job. The company had increased sales revenue by almost 50 percent. Additionally, David was well liked and respected by most of the employees and other officers in the company. In addition to doing an excellent job in the roles he had held since joining the business, he had developed a good rapport with most of the executive team, department heads, and plant supervisors. He demonstrated an open, flexible leadership style and often combined collaborative approaches with strong problem-solving skills to encourage others and promote the success of the company.

David seemed well qualified to move into the CEO position when his father retired. Moreover, he had groomed a qualified successor to assume his role as VP of sales and marketing. During his father's retirement party, most of the employees turned out to wish him well; David felt confident he would be able to make the transition into the new role smoothly. Additionally, his father would remain as chairman of the board and come into the plant a few hours a week. Two of the other vice presidents, one for finance and one for operations, were older and had been in the business since its founding over thirty years earlier; they were also remaining to ensure a smooth transition. David also expected the vice president of engineering and his new vice president of sales and marketing to be stabilizing factors in the transition.

About four months into his new role as CEO, David began to perceive some challenges he had not anticipated. Though he demonstrated a highly collaborative leadership style, he often made a decision that the others on his executive team did not agree with; they would go to his father to gain his support in attempting to reverse David's decision. Additionally, David perceived that executive team members, including the vice president of engineering, seemed to operate independently, without showing the same deference to David as they did to his father. David was even more perplexed when he learned that the VP of engineering and the new VP of sales and marketing were working closely together on new product ideas, without David's input.

As a result of the direction of the executive team, David grew uncomfortable with his new role and wanted to consider options for strengthening his leadership position.

1. What may be contributing to David's discomfort?
2. List reasonable options that David may consider to strengthen his leadership position.
3. What would you do in David's position?
4. What are the pros and cons inherent in your choice of action?

Case Two. Who's in Charge?

For more than three years, Taylor has been a successful project leader in the client services department of Collins and Thompson, a marketing firm in Los Angeles. Collins and Thompson is a medium-sized organization that provides business-to-business marketing services and programs. Its clients include professional services firms: accountants, management consultants, lawyers, commercial real estate firms, and IT services contractors.

Taylor's team is responsible for developing and delivering new marketing programs to promote business-to-business sales for clients in the greater Los Angeles area. She is well respected by her seven team members and is one of three project leaders who could replace Tom, the director of creative services, when he moves to another position.

Heading a highly talented and creative team, Taylor has found that she needs to flex her natural directive and task-focused style to a more participative approach. This leadership style seems to work well for Taylor's highly competent and committed team. She has also adapted her style by affording most of her team reasonable levels of autonomy and responsibility without having to demonstrate as much structure and direction as she normally would with a less talented group.

Terri was recently added to Taylor's team; she was formerly the marketing director from one of Collins and Thompson's competitors. Terri was considered overqualified for serving in a project team role, but she became available when her firm was acquired by a larger marketing company that put one of its staff members in her position. Because of Terri's outstanding credentials and the fact that executives at Collins and Thompson believe she'll be an excellent asset at a higher level when available, she was hired and placed on Taylor's team for the interim.

While Taylor appreciates having such a talented and experienced member on her team, she has found the situation difficult to manage. Terri does not seem to respect Taylor's role as the team leader. She often critiques Taylor, who is younger and less experienced, in front of other team members. Because Terri has a strong perfectionist style and significantly more experience, Taylor has tried to accept her feedback. But recently, Terri has also begun to overstep Taylor's leadership role by providing more informal guidance to other team members.

Taylor is hesitant to go to Tom, her supervisor, for assistance in regards to Terri, for a couple of reasons. First, she knows that Terri will likely not remain on her team for long because the company plans to advance her soon when a more senior role becomes available. Terri could one day be above Taylor, which could affect her career path. Second, Taylor does not want to appear incapable of managing a strong and highly experienced professional such as Terri, as she hopes to move up as well when the opportunity becomes available.

1. What factors are contributing to the leadership challenge Taylor is facing?
2. What are the most reasonable options for Taylor to consider in handling the challenge?
3. What would you do in Taylor's position?
4. What risks and opportunities may result from your choice of action?

Case 3. Teens over the Edge

Dillon's sister is a member of the girl's high school basketball team. The team has made it to the state quarterfinal playoffs. As part of a student government project, Dillon has organized a group of students to attend the team's game, traveling by bus. On the evening of their trip to the game, it's snowing. The playoff site is over forty miles from their hometown.

On the way, the bus skids and slides off the icy road. It careens over an embankment into a ravine, where it is not visible from the road. The embankment is quite steep and icy; it would be extremely difficult to climb out in the dark. The motor and the electricity on the bus are out. The driver is unconscious. The only light available comes from students' cell phones. However, none of the phones has service.

The bus holds about forty students, ages twelve to eighteen. Initially, no one other than the driver seems to be seriously injured, although some students have cuts and bruises. There is a lot of confusion; some students are laughing and joking while others are emotionally upset and expressing their fears. Because there is no light outside the vehicle and it is snowing hard, it is almost impossible to determine how far the bus is from the road. A stiff wind accompanies the snow, and the temperature is below freezing.

Seventeen-year-old Dillon is physically small and naturally introverted. As a new member of the student government, he is not completely sure of his leadership role in this situation. But because he organized the trip, he feels a significant measure of responsibility to respond to the emergency. It is freezing cold outside of the bus, the driver is unconscious and cannot act, and there is obviously danger to the students. Dillon feels responsible and believes he should step up and take a leadership role.

1. If you were in Dillon's place, what is likely to be your *first* action after determining the driver is unconscious?
2. What steps would you take to bring order to the entire group?
3. What else should you accomplish within the first few minutes after the accident?
4. What will be your actions if it appears no emergency assistance is coming to provide help?

Case 4. Filling Her Own Shoes

Carrie has served admirably as the CEO of the nonprofit organization she founded over twenty years ago. The organization provides Big Brother—and Big Sister-type services to underprivileged children in a large Midwestern city. While she feels a great attachment to the organization she has led successfully through difficult times, health issues just recently surfaced that require her to identify a successor. Her physicians strongly advise that she leave the organization within three months.

Carrie is aware that survival is becoming a greater concern for nonprofits like hers in today's difficult economic environment. Similar organizations are all competing for shrinking funding sources with much larger organizations that have greater political interests and ties. Critical issues such as managing change, working with the board of directors, identifying new sources of revenue, and retaining committed staff and volunteer corps are more challenging than ever. It will take a very talented and experienced person to step into her position and handle the transition successfully. Furthermore, it may be relatively expensive to bring someone in from the outside, especially if they are not a local resident.

Like all good leaders, Carrie has always been well aware of the importance of grooming successors from within. But the surprise dilemma of having to leave relatively soon has caught her without anyone she feels is ready to assume the broad span of leadership challenges the position holds. Two current executives are interested in assuming her position and believe they are qualified. One is the controller, who is a good manager but knows little about leading or managing beyond the scope of his current financial responsibilities. The other is the vice president for human resources, who is well connected and may be able to do an excellent job of fund raising but does not demonstrate much understanding of how to handle strategic issues.

As she ponders how to go about solving this especially difficult dilemma, Carrie feels overwhelmed. Not only is her health a major issue, but her organization is in a precarious position. The difficult economic times coupled with her desire to avoid alienating two staff members who want to assume her role by bringing in an outsider are weighing heavily upon her as she considers her options.

1. What are the most critical issues Carrie must address immediately?
2. How should she handle the interest in her position as expressed by the controller and vice president of human resources?
3. What are the most important qualifications she should seek in her replacement?
4. Briefly list steps she may consider to manage the transition until a successor has been hired.

CHAPTER 10

APPLICATION

I hope the case studies in chapter 9 were constructive in revisiting some of the concepts developed in the previous eight chapters. Perhaps you had the opportunity to discuss the cases with others. Discussing the issues described in the cases should promote learning, aid in concept retention, and add to the value of the reading and participation in the online assessments. However, if you are currently in a leadership role that enables you to apply some of the information I have covered, you will receive far more value than just engaging in basic study or discussing the case studies. If you are not currently in a formal leadership role, I still recommend looking for opportunities to use the content you found of interest in everyday interaction with others, whenever practical.

In order to apply information that you believe has value, I suggest using a technique that has proven useful to many of my clients: the proven approach of goal setting.[73] Let's begin by revisiting steps described in chapter 3 that are necessary to apply a new skill or behavior when learning to become a better leader:

1. There must be a *good reason* to learn a new behavior or skill.
2. Learners must be introduced to appropriate skills or techniques they *want* to apply.
3. Learners must *apply* the skill or technique regularly as practical.
4. *Visualizing* and keeping sight of value while using the skill or technique is essential.
5. To ensure that the new skill becomes automatic, success must be achieved.

Chapters 1 through 8 addressed the first two steps. In this chapter, we will address steps three and four, which require disciplined practice in a practical setting and staying mindful of the value of success. In order to achieve this, you'll need to do a few things that will help you make practical use of what you have learned. I'll begin by suggesting some approaches for you to identify content from the chapters that is more likely to have value for you. Then I'll suggest methods for application and ways to reinforce and review results.

I.   Selecting the Right Goals to Apply Learning

Briefly review those chapters or sections that were most interesting to you. The summary points at the end of each chapter can help you recall the most central lessons from the chapter. Do this with the goal of identifying specific information, tools, or techniques you can apply to your current circumstances. As suggested earlier, if possible, gain the perspective of others when identifying areas to work on. The input of people you interact with is essential when establishing priorities for what you ought to address in leadership contexts.

As you review the chapters, attempt to identify a group of no more than three concepts or lessons from the entire book that you believe will have value in your current leadership role, job, or life situation. You may choose them all from one chapter or pick them from different chapters. Selecting more than three may become complicated because it can dissipate the focus required to adopt them as part of your normal behavior.

Later after successful application of those three you may identify more. Prior to performing this step, in addition to review of the chapter content also review each of the self-rating exercises you completed (such as the ULQ, LSI, LBI, or MBI). They may be particularly helpful in identification of skills, behaviors or broader goals you will want to work on. After you have successfully applied the first group of three behaviors, activities or goals, you may decide to do more.

I call this approach an "application plan." I have used it successfully in coaching a large number of people over many years. After using it for a reasonable period of time, most people permanently change their leadership behavior for the better. In essence, it is no more than goal setting combined with disciplined follow-through to ensure application. However, while relatively simple, it is systematic enough to ensure that achieving these goals will improve how you lead.

Furthermore, the value of identifying and then writing down goals that you will stay mindful of is an unexcelled tool for ensuring constructive results. In his classic self-help work on success, *Think and Grow Rich*, Napoleon Hill makes a strong and convincing case for the value of goal setting and regular reading and focus on them to ensure results. Though a central theme in Hill's book is how to accumulate wealth, the principles for leading are an outstanding guide for self-development of leadership skills. *Think and Grow Rich*, is arguably the most well known motivational book of the twentieth century. The principles described in Hill's book are likely to have significant value for anyone who wants to increase their leadership potential in any setting.[74]

Keep in mind that broad or ambiguous goals without a specific focus tend to have limited value. A more targeted approach with a specific plan for applying your goals will yield much better results. So your application plan should focus on very specific behaviors or activities and a well-defined context in which to apply them. Choosing ambiguous goals can actually work in reverse and hinder improvement.

For instance, many people set New Year's resolutions without developing a realistic plan to achieve them. Such resolutions often amount to little more than temporary efforts. Examples of such resolutions include losing weight, saving more from earnings, quitting smoking, behaving differently with others, and becoming more organized. But too often the resolutions are soon forgotten, resulting in no benefit. There are several reasons such goal setting exercises rarely succeed: lack of focus, lack of discipline, no practical method to follow through, or even the wrong goal to begin with.

Here is a very common case of the wrong goal to begin with: Harold states on December 31, "I'm going to lose fifty pounds by May 1." The goal may be motivated by a recommendation from his physician, or maybe Harold simply does not like the way he looks and feels anymore. While Harold's goal of losing weight by a certain date may sound constructive, it might not actually address a more critical issue: an unhealthy lifestyle that lacks proper nutrition and regular exercise. Going on a temporary diet to lose fifty pounds is likely to yield only temporary results if any. Actually, Harold needs to do something far more significant than just lose weight: He needs to concentrate on a *lasting* lifestyle change to become fit and healthy.

Following a popular diet or using a weight loss product may actually work against Harold. In his case, they offer only a symbolic quick fix to make him feel like he's doing something beneficial. In fact, he's doing very little other than spending money or going through temporary motions. Even if he does drop some weight, he may gain even more back when he reverts to his old lifestyle, which is what he actually needed to change to begin with. He hasn't addressed the root problem: his need for better nutrition and regular exercise.

Harold doesn't need to buy any quick fix products or purchase a fitness club membership to become more healthy. However, he does need to make a major lifestyle change for the better and demonstrate enough *self-discipline* to make it last. Changing deeply engrained lifestyle behaviors, such as learning to eat right and get regular exercise, can be very difficult for some people.

Harold's case illustrates a common mistake that people often make when trying to become a better leader: choosing the wrong goal to begin and not making a consistent effort to change. Let's consider Barbara, a manager in a professional services business. She perceives she has less than satisfactory rapport with many of her staff. As a result, she desires to strengthen her leadership abilities by becoming better at communicating. She decides to enroll in a one-day communications seminar that teaches participants how to become better at listening and building rapport.

However, her real problem—the lack of enough one-on-one time with her staff—is not likely to be corrected by attending a seminar on communications. Again, as with Harold's diet, she may feel a symbolic satisfaction of doing something when she signs up for the seminar. However, if the change she hopes to promote does not focus specifically on the real need and lacks a systematic follow-through, there will be very little value for her.

It might be better for Barbara to first gather input on what she needs from a credible source in her office. If she does this, she may learn quickly that just budgeting some regular time for a few of her key team members can do more to improve her relationships than attending a seminar.

Excellent leaders never quit growing and improving their leadership abilities. And people who continually grow as leaders are very open to valid input from others. They are objective about their needs, learn from their mistakes, and regularly strive to become better. Such habits enable them to improve. If you want to strengthen your leadership abilities by using some of what we have covered, get input from others who know you well before selecting your initial goals.

You may initially decide to have an open dialogue with a credible person who is familiar with your leadership behavior first hand in respect to how you can grow as a leader. After that discussion, you should review the learning points from each chapter and then select a few for consideration. At that point, you may want further input before narrowing your focus down to near-term goals and priorities for strengthening your leadership ability.

II. Your Application Plan

You may decide on your own how and where to apply what you find valuable in this book. It is not absolutely necessary to use the plan I will prescribe. However, the structured application program I will describe has worked well with hundreds of my clients and students over many years. It includes the following steps:

- Write down the concepts you believe will have the most *tangible* value now
- Translate the concepts into goals, including the *context* in which they apply
- Define specific behaviors or activities that will *operationalize* your goals
- Perform the activities as *regularly* as practical
- *Measure* the results and *reinforce* them

Step One. Write down the concepts you believe will have the most tangible value now.

Review the summary points at the end of each chapter. Also review the results of any assessment exercises you completed to identify areas for improvement. Keep in mind that if you try to do too many new things at one time, you are less likely to be successful at any one of them. With advice from a credible source, prioritize what you want to work on in the near term. Focus on what is most pressing in the here and now. Later, you can choose other goals after you have made progress on what is most important now.

Step Two. Translate the concepts into goals, including the context in which they apply.

Once you have identified concepts you think will have the most value for the near term and gained objective perspective from a credible source, you will need to set the context for application. For example, if you are certain that becoming a better listener will strengthen your leadership ability, you must determine ways to improve that skill in which you can assess specific results. Because improving your listening skills requires changing a deeply engrained behavior, it's going to require more focus than an easier goal such as learning to budget more time for organization and planning.

Just deciding to listen better is probably too broad a goal to accomplish much. Furthermore, attempting to measure the results of such an ambiguous goal is impractical. It would be better to identify the context for this application. In this example, you might say, "Improve my focus when listening in Friday morning staff meetings." This will provide a specific context that is easier to remember and will focus more upon observable improvement.

Step Three. Define specific behaviors or activities that will operationalize your goals.

The goal itself is still only a reference to an *outcome*. What must be performed to achieve the outcome? It requires defining specific behaviors or activities in order to ensure application. In addition, it also requires reviewing the results and measuring them. If possible, identify someone who will be impacted by the activities. With the goal of becoming a better listener in Friday morning staff meetings, the behaviors might include the following:

- Take notes and ask questions to ensure understanding when Carrie, Thomas, and Ricky provide updates on the week's activities.
- When I am defining the next week's activities, encourage questions and listen closely when asked to ensure adequate response.
- Budget enough time for each of our staff to express appropriate concerns.

What if your goal is to become more decisive? Again, you'll have to identify a context and the kinds of activities that you must perform to be more decisive. As the Leadership Behavior Index (used in

Exercise #3 at the end of chapter 4) illustrates, specific activities for decision making may include:

- Consider a variety of view points before decisions when possible and practical
- Seek rational options despite emotional considerations when making decisions
- Be able to make quick decisions when necessary

Such a focused approach may seem more structured and detailed than necessary or practical. However, without identifying just what you have to do differently and where, there's a good chance you won't really do anything differently and you won't improve very much. At the very least, identify the context and functions where you will apply the technique.

Step Four. Perform the activities as regularly as practical.

This step requires that you remain conscious of your goals. Some people actually print them out and display them as a reminder. Others input them into a computer program or on their iPad to monitor their progress. A good approach is to discuss your progress with a mentor, associate, or friend. But remember that if you do not use *something* to remind you to stay focused and disciplined with the application, it's very possible your goals will soon be forgotten. This can happen as you become preoccupied with daily duties and responsibilities that can make you forget about long-term development goals.

Step Five. Measure the results and reinforce them.

Self-rating at regular intervals is an excellent way to remind yourself to apply learning as you work on your goals. I also suggest soliciting input from others as to how you are doing. You may decide to use a simple numerical score or make notes on your progress and discuss them with a colleague. But do remember that *objective* measurement of progress is one of the most important learning tools. It promotes focus, can help redirect efforts where necessary, and reinforces results. It may take weeks (or even months) of application until the change you seek becomes a habit, so stay with it. Anything worthwhile takes work and discipline.

How much time it takes to learn new leadership skills varies widely, depending upon a number of factors. Learning basic organizational skills obviously takes less time than becoming skilled at conflict resolution. And of course the amount of time and focus invested will impact the time required. Various studies suggest that it can take anywhere from a couple of weeks to many months, depending upon the circumstances and other variables

Experts on behavioral change often say that overwriting old behaviors is a formidable challenge; it can be the most significant factor when learning new behaviors. PsyBlog.com, Redbird Communications, LucReid.com, and other such organizations that perform behavioral research maintain that acquiring any new behavior typically requires a great amount of disciplined practice with appropriate reinforcement.

According to research by Phillippa Lally and colleagues from the Cancer Research and Health Behavior Center, based at UCL in the United Kingdom,[75] it can take a couple of months to form a new habit. The study by Lally's team looked at how people form habits and was published in the *European Journal of Social Psychology*. She explains the key factors in creating and breaking habits and how we can help establish new patterns of behavior:

> *In our study, we looked at how long it took people to reach a limit of self-reported automaticity for performing an initially new behavior (that is, performing an action automatically), and the average time (among those for whom our model was a good fit) was 66 days . . . . Habits are behaviors which are performed automatically because they have been performed frequently in the past. This repetition creates a mental association between the situation (cue) and action (behavior) which means that when the cue is encountered the behavior*

> *is performed automatically. Automaticity has a number of components, one of which is lack of thought.*

That may seem daunting, but don't let it keep you from working at becoming better at leading. Remember the case of Barbara, who desired to strengthen communications with her team? That was actually just a matter of identifying a solution that did not require a major behavior change on her part. It simply required budgeting more time to interact with some of her key staff. In fact, learning to lead better in many cases has more to do with knowing *how* and *where* to invest more time and effort than attempting to make a significant behavioral change.

However, changes such as improving your listening skills take more time and effort, but they are well worth it. Personal communications behavior such as listening effectively, which is largely a function of habit, is a critical skill required for successful interactions with others. And in direct contact contexts, where most leadership roles occur, interactive skills are absolutely essential.

III. Long-Term Application

Whether you use the application plan approach I have described or your own goal setting methods, you will have acquired an approach for growth that can help with other goals throughout your life. Those goals may be related to leadership, management, or *any* role where you interact with others. Keep in mind that one of the most important ingredients for growth is *self-discipline*. Without self-discipline and the effort and persistence required to learn new skills, little real growth is likely to occur.

I always encourage everyone I work with who wants to become better at leading to focus their effort on *applying* what they learn, rather than just learning *about* leadership concepts. Books, seminars, and leadership resources have little value if you do not use what you learn.

The application approach I have described also has value when coaching and developing others. For example, if you are helping team members learn how to supervise more effectively, you will want to begin by working with them to identify techniques that will actually apply to their specific context. And as illustrated earlier, broad and ambiguous goals are not likely to yield results. Help them identify near-term developmental priorities that they recognize as valuable. If they don't see the value to begin with, growth will probably not result.

Because good leaders are in a constant state of growth, they tend to seek new sources of learning continually. They may do this by reading, participating in seminars, taking courses, accessing online educational resources, and using other practical means. However, without effectively applying what they learn, they risk becoming "information junkies" who know a lot *about* many things, but little about *how to* do them. Goal setting, whether with the suggested application plan or some other approach to ensure follow-through, is indispensible.

EPILOGUE

As asserted at the beginning of this book, the greater a person's ability to lead the greater will be their likelihood of success in all aspects of their life. *There is no better advantage for success in life than the ability to lead.* No amount of education, economic resources, or network of friends can surpass the value of knowing how to lead effectively.

All sophisticated cultures continuously seek new and better ways of doing things. It is the leaders who identify them and shows the way. They may do this formally with authority or informally without authority. Regardless, they do it through their own initiative, sense of responsibility and desire to serve. That is what makes them leaders. Practically any person can strengthen their ability to lead through application of the same principles.

The illustrations of the principle-based leaders we have examined demonstrate that such outstanding people in addition to initiative, responsibility and the desire to serve learned

> *There is no better advantage for success in life than the ability to lead.*

how to demonstrate vision, character, excellent problem solving and decision skills and the ability to relate well to others. This formula for leadership success applies in any circumstance in which people come together for a common goal or purpose.

The path we have pursued in building your leadership abilities is an integrated process. Every step outlined is necessary for it to yield significant benefit. If you begin with a definite purpose of strengthening your leadership ability, perform objective self-assessment, identify areas for improvement, share your discoveries and developmental needs with others and follow through on specific well conceived goals, you will become much more effective as a leader. And you may become an outstanding leader on the level of those men and women we have profiled.

You are invited to seek additional leadership perspective and resources by going to GreenbrierLeadership.com. All of us involved in the Greenbrier Leadership Institute will consider it a privilege to respond to your questions or needs in whatever way we can to serve you.

THE GREENBRIER LEADERSHIP INSTITUTE

The Greenbrier Leadership Institute was initiated in 2008 and formalized with its own charter through the Greenbrier Military School Alumni Association in 2009. The institute is a continuation of a long heritage of leadership development begun by Greenbrier Military School (GMS). The institute was created and is staffed by graduates of Greenbrier Military School in the interest of continuing the educational legacy of leadership established by GMS over its illustrious 160-year history.

Greenbrier Military School was a private military boarding high school for young men, located in Lewisburg, West Virginia. It also offered a one-year post-high school college preparatory program. The school began in 1812 when Dr. John McElhenney founded the Lewisburg Academy for boys and girls. Eventually, both the Greenbrier College for Women and Greenbrier Military School evolved from the original Lewisburg Academy.

The modern Greenbrier Military School was run by the Moore family until its closing in 1972. The school became one of the premier military schools for high school students in the United States. The college preparatory program was popular with military schools during that period and continues so today. At one point, GMS had over four hundred students from seventh grade through the postgraduate program.

Greenbrier Military School was renowned for developing excellence, achievement, and leadership characteristics in its graduates. The academic program, athletic program, excellent leadership development through the military training, and even the marching band were hallmarks of the superior education offered by the school. An unusually high proportion of GMS graduates went on to outstanding success in their careers.

Though the school closed its doors in 1972, the educational tradition of leadership and service continues today through the Greenbrier Leadership Institute. From its inception, the impact of the institute has grown steadily. Today, the institute offers video-based leadership education, numerous live programs for adults and students, written resources, and online leadership education through GreenbrierLeadership.com.

The mission of the Greenbrier Leadership Institute is to develop principle-based leaders for the twenty-first century in public and private sectors. Principle-based leaders are men and women whose leadership influence is founded upon integrity, service, and character. The Greenbrier Leadership Institute also provides most of its programs to the public at large, at no charge.

MOST PREFERRED LEADER SURVEY

Greenbrier
Leadership Institute

Effective leadership may be demonstrated in formal or informal settings. The following questions will ask you about a person in a leadership role with whom you have had direct experience. You may choose someone from a formal supervisory or professional setting, or a person outside a supervisory setting (such as a teacher, coach, etc.) However, choose someone who was most able to gain your respect and commitment toward specific and worthwhile goals or results.

Who was the person that had the most positive impact upon you as a leader and what was the context in which the leader influenced you for the better?

_____

_____

_____

_____

Explain why this person was so effective with you and include specific examples.

_____

_____

_____

_____

What positive achievements or outcomes did this person's influence result in for you?

_____

_____

_____

_____

What specific activities did this person perform that provided value for you or others?

_____

_____

_____

_____

What characteristics or abilities did this person demonstrate that you aspire to emulate?

_____

_____

_____

_____

ADDITIONAL LEADERSHIP DEVELOPMENT RESOURCES

The following includes additional information about leadership development experts, credible books on leadership or related topics, and a list of important leadership theories that are good supplements to what has been covered in this book.

Leadership Experts

1. John C. Maxwell (http://www.johnmaxwell.com) is unquestionably one of the most respected leadership development professionals; his methods are recognized internationally as having outstanding value across all leadership arenas.
2. Ken Blanchard (http://kenblanchard.com) co-wrote (with Spencer Johnson) *The One Minute Manager,* which has sold over thirteen million copies and has been translated into thirty-seven languages. He has coauthored over thirty other best-selling books. Along with Paul Hersey, who developed the concept of situational leadership, Dr. Blanchard has become an icon of contemporary leadership development theories and programs.
3. Warren G. Bennis (http://warrenbennis.com) is highly esteemed American scholar, organizational consultant, and author; he is widely regarded as a pioneer in contemporary leadership studies. Bennis is a distinguished professor of business administration and the founding chairman

of the Leadership Institute at the University of Southern California.

4. Tony Dungy (http://www.coachdungy.com) originally gained leadership fame as a Super Bowl—winning coach in 2007. Soon after that, he began to earn recognition as an outstanding speaker, author, and advisor on leadership principles. He is one of the most sought after speakers on leadership issues today.

5. Ram Charan (http://www.ram-charan.com) is a highly respected and one of the top business advisors and executive coaches in the world today. His clients include numerous Fortune 100 companies and corporate organizations around the globe. He is a well known author and speaker on leadership principles that apply in all settings.

6. Meg Whitman (http://www.makers.com/meg-whitman), president and chief executive officer of Hewlett-Packard, joins an exclusive group of women CEOs in America. Her views and publications on leadership are highly sought in all sectors of the business community.

7. Mark Driscoll (http://marshill.com/pastors/mark-driscoll) is currently one of the most highly quoted experts on leadership; he has written books and articles on business, faith-based organizations, marriage and family, and lifelong achievement.

8. Jack Welsh (http://jackwelch.strayer.edu/about/jack-welch) is a successful author and speaker on leadership topics. His meteoric rise to prominence as a highly respected expert on leadership began as the result of his outstanding performance as the CEO of General Electric.

9. Tom Peters (http://www.tompeters.com) first gained a national reputation as an expert on the topic of leadership with his best selling *In Search of Excellence*, written with coauthor Bob Waterman. Since the 1980s, Peters has continued to write, speak, and consult on leadership issues with top CEOs worldwide.

10. Marshal Goldsmith (http://www.marshallgoldsmithlibrary. com) is an author and speaker on various leadership topics. He initially gained attention in pioneering work in using

"360 degree feedback" for managers to gain an objective perspective from their staff on what they can do to improve their leadership capabilities.

Books on Leadership Development and Related Topics

On Becoming a Leader. In this book, Warren G. Bennis provides timeless and practical lessons on leadership principles. The book has recently been updated for tomorrow's leaders, with a new introduction by the author.

Leadership 2.0. Describes the concepts of Adaptive Leadership in a practical, hands-on manner. The authors, Travis Bradberry and Jean Greaves are well known and highly respected for their research on how to develop leaders.

Wooden on Leadership: How to Create a Winning Organization. John Wooden, Hall of Fame basketball coach at UCLA, describes principles and methods for leading outstanding teams that apply in business settings.

Cognitive Harmony: An Adventure in Mental Fitness. Jerry Stocking illustrates various techniques for increasing cognitive awareness and skills that will strengthen a leader's ability to relate to and develop others. Furthermore, Stocking addresses numerous ways leaders can improve their perception assessing others and become better at reading nonverbal messages.

How to Grow Leaders: The Seven Key Principles of Effective Development. Leadership development expert John Adair identifies seven principles that apply to developing leadership qualities and abilities; this book is very appropriate for leaders in corporate as well as public sector environments.

Thinking Fast and Slow. Nobel Prize laureate Daniel Kahneman provides deep insight into why people behave the way they do, including making decisions, relating to others, and pursuing goals.

This outstanding book provides a wealth of knowledge on how the human mind works, which can benefit leaders at any level.

The 21 Irrefutable Laws of Leadership: Follow Them and People Will Follow You. John C. Maxwell provides a blueprint of indispensible guidelines that enable leaders to promote influence balanced with results that apply in all leadership contexts.

The Million Dollar Hire: Build Your Bottom Line One Employee at a Time. David P. Jones describes essential techniques for recruiting and selecting top talent as well as principles for laying the groundwork to turn outstanding hires into outstanding leaders. Dr. Jones provides a blueprint for the most critical qualities, including leadership potential that organizations should look for before any hiring decision.

The Center for Creative Leadership Handbook of Leadership Development. Editors Eleanor Van Velsor, Cynthia D. McCauley, and Marian N. Ruderman have put together one of the most practical and comprehensive packages of resources for building outstanding leadership in any organization.

Remarkable Leadership: Unleashing Your Leadership Potential One Skill at a Time. Kevin Eikenberry does an excellent job of describing practical methods to transfer principles of effective leadership into everyday leadership contexts.

Classic Leadership Theories

These are some of the more prominent theories that have contributed significantly to leadership development efforts over the past seventy-five years. Studying them will provide a background on important work that has served to advance understanding of effective leadership practices.

> ➢ Trait Theory: Gordon Allport
> ➢ Theory Y and Theory X: Douglas MacGregor

- ➢ The Ohio State Studies: R. M. Stogdill and A. E. Coons
- ➢ University of Michigan Studies: Rensis Likert
- ➢ The "Managerial Grid": Robert R. Blake and Jane Mouton
- ➢ Contingency Model of Leadership: Fred Fiedler
- ➢ Life Cycle Theory of Leadership (Situational): Paul Hersey and Kenneth Blanchard
- ➢ Transactional and Transformational Leadership: James MacGregor Burns
- ➢ Principle-Centered Leadership: Steven R. Covey

NOTES FOR CASE STUDIES

Considerations for Case 1, "The Heir Apparent"

Formal assumption of a new leadership role does not automatically afford anyone all of the authority or influence that a genuine leader must earn to be effective. Though David is qualified and well liked, and he has contributed much to the success of the business, assuming the role after the retirement of his father did not guarantee him complete support.

It usually takes time to earn the genuine role of leader in many people's eyes. People do not become a true leader until they are ratified in the hearts and minds of their subordinates. That occurs as people develop respect for their abilities and see them as an appropriate leader. That normally takes time and must be solidified with a demonstration of *competence*. It does not occur immediately and cannot be rushed.

Furthermore, being the son of the founder and CEO and having been identified as the likely new CEO may have built in some special obstacles for David. Though he is popular, there may be some resentment or even jealousy in some others in the organization. If so, that could contribute to the challenges David perceives at the four-month point in his new role.

David's leadership style proved effective as vice president of sales and marketing. However, it's obvious that his new role increases the demand for demonstrating authority across the entire organization, and this may require a little more assertiveness. While that does not necessitate David becoming an authoritarian leader, it does mean that he must demonstrate an additional level of assertiveness where appropriate.

If he increases his assertiveness now, it should be done in a tactful but firm manner with a few key individuals. And rather than attempting to sway them with an overt appeal to his formal authority as CEO, he should use finesse and work *with* them rather than *over* them to involve each of his senior people in his decision making. Booker T. Washington's approach, as described in chapter 8, illustrates the point. Washington often had to sway both allies *and* opponents with a combination of finesse, reason, and leverage to win support for his decisions. His actions were always conducted in a firm but tactful manner.

It's also obvious in David's case that being an effective leader requires much more than just applying an appropriate leadership style. Additionally, his values, the values of others, and their individual goals all must factor into how he leads. For example, if he is finding it difficult to gain consensus on a decision he is responsible for, he should assess what is at the core of the resistance. That does not mean that he has to succumb to their will, but it does mean that more open dialogue and mutual problem solving and strategy formulation may be appropriate.

Additionally, role considerations may be contributing to David's perceived challenges. The two senior vice presidents were supportive of David's father from the beginning. But even though he is now only chairman of the board, that will not automatically change how they see him. Though he is no longer working in their presence on a regular basis, the senior VPs may still feel that he is ultimately the final "go to" individual for the direction of the business.

It's also possible that the vice president of engineering may be spending more time brainstorming product ideas with the new VP of sales and marketing only because David is not as available as before. David should not assume there is any more to the situation, until he knows more about what the two are working on. And he never will until he purposefully engages with the key players and listens to their perspectives.

David has a number of reasonable options to consider. They include the following:

1. Speak with his father about how he interacts with members of the executive group. Part of that dialogue may be to request more support and deference to his new position as CEO. That would especially apply when others attempt to gain the chairman's support to override decisions that David has made.
2. Use more engagement and regular communication with key executive team members as necessary to build respect for his abilities as the CEO. To accomplish this, David will need to demonstrate value in his role as leader by helping them be more successful in *their* roles. His actions will speak far louder than his words in this respect.
3. David must be patient and recognize that the best natural leadership roles evolve, given time. David is only four months into the position. It will take time to build an accepted leadership role with his executives. And that will be a function of the principles that guide how he leads as well as the ultimate value he demonstrates through his actions.

There are, of course, many other options David may consider. These three can be addressed in the near term. Additional options may arise as things change and other situations occur. David must keep in mind the need to be flexible but firm as he becomes more familiar with his new role. His confidence in his new role should grow as a result of his competence and the value others see in him.

Considerations for Case 2, "Who's in Charge?"

Placing a highly experienced professional under the authority of a much less experienced leader is a recipe for significant problems. Though Collins and Thompson executives may have been wise to hire Terri, the position they chose for her was not the best way to transition her into the business. They overlooked the fact that a significant requirement for leaders to be effective is that they must have the knowledge and experience to provide credible guidance to those within their span of authority. Leaders do not have to know more than each team member, but they must know enough to be able to provide competent direction and support.

In this situation, Taylor is disadvantaged in her leadership role not being as experienced or knowledgeable as Terri. However, Taylor is the project team leader, and Terri is under her authority. Because of that, Taylor can't relinquish the primary leadership role to Terri without eroding her credibility and losing control of the direction of the team. If Taylor intends to remain the leader, she will have to take action to change the direction of the group dynamic and the roles she and Terri play in respect to each other.

If Taylor allows the fear of being perceived negatively to keep from speaking to Tom about the dilemma, she is very likely cutting herself off from a constructive source of help. It's possible there could be someone above her in the hierarchy that understands the situation and can help. Even if that were not the case, there is no shame in inquiring. The unsound management decision to place Terri under Taylor is not a reflection on Taylor.

An additional consideration is Taylor's leadership style. While her most natural style would be *directive*, she has recently become much more flexible by allowing her team members greater autonomy and freedom. But now that she has a strong perfectionist and highly experienced team member, who may one day be her superior, she will be pushed even further against her most natural style if she conciliates any more. This can be very stressful.

If Taylor continues to react to Terri on a day-to-day basis with the hope that Terri is moved elsewhere, Taylor's leadership role will continue to erode. Taylor will have to take constructive action to change the direction of the situation now. She must also consider that if she elects to deal directly with Terri on the matter, she will have to be very careful in her approach.

Taylor might attempt to assert her authority over Terri, but that raises another issue. The authority of most leaders comes from the consent of those they lead. Taylor obviously does not possess that level of authority in this situation with Terri. So she would have to try to *force* her authority upon Terri, and that may have more negative repercussions than it's worth.

On the other hand, if Taylor were to initiate a discussion with Terri about the dilemma and make it clear that the two of them must resolve the issue *together*, she may be on firmer ground. This is especially true if Taylor makes it clear she is involving Terri in identifying options and weighing their merits. Being more experienced, Terri might recognize that it is in everyone's best interest, including her own, that they work it out. If she doesn't, then Taylor has at least offered a constructive option that demonstrates a mature approach; this may garner respect from Terri and support from Tom.

Another option for Taylor is to demonstrate a firmer response to Terri, incident by incident, when she tries to critique her or oversteps her leadership role with individual team members. Depending upon the situation and persons involved, Taylor must keep certain appropriate leadership principles in mind to guide her actions. In this case, that means she needs to stay confident in her role and mindful of what is best for her team. She must maintain her dignity by being patient and at the same time treat Terri in a professional manner by communicating openly and honestly.

Taylor need not relinquish her leadership role because of this difficult challenge. Leaders *are* leaders more so by their actions and intentions than by their words. And as long as they hold the formal position no one can strip them of their leadership *role* unless they permit it. Taylor will more likely remain strong in her leadership role by stepping up to the challenge and either working with Terri to identify constructive options or working without Terri to maintain her influence with the other team members.

Considerations for Case 3, "Teens over the Edge"

Dillon has no formal leadership role. However, because he arranged the trip, he feels compelled to take responsibility. It is obvious that someone must pull together the other teens and assess the situation.

Dillon may not attempt to assume any formal authority. Instead, his natural instincts may be to take action in either directing or helping facilitate a group of the most responsible and mature students to come together quickly. In that group, it's likely a natural dynamic will form that will reveal who is best suited to assume the central leadership position. It is possible there may also be co-leaders with appropriate abilities that may step forward.

Whether Dillon or someone else becomes the primary leader, the priorities and tasks at hand will be the same. Once a leadership group with responsible members is formed, it must then assess the critical issues. These include attending to the driver, checking the others for serious injuries, calming the students who are frightened, finding an emergency first aid kit, and making sure there is no threat of fire or other crash-related issues.

Dillon must quickly assess the potential knowledge, skills, and abilities of other team members to decide who will be responsible for what activity. Some students might have first aid experience, some may be suited for reassuring the others; another may have mechanical skills that could be used. It is paramount, however, that the leader demonstrates calm and confident leadership.

Another important decision must be made: whether someone should attempt to climb back up to the highway and seek help. Because of the wintery conditions and the lack of visibility, that could be very dangerous. This decision requires a thorough assessment of the elements as well as the skills of the students who are willing to attempt it. Another concern is whether there are any emergency tools on board the bus that can be used.

The available resources on the bus and the capabilities of the teens will ultimately determine the leader's decisions. As was illustrated in chapter 1 when Captain Sullenberger had to overcome fear and act quickly, Dillon will have to weigh a number of options and risks related to the safety of others. In this case, our teenage leader may by necessity face similar challenges.

Considerations for Case 4, "Filling Her Own Shoes"

To be effective, nonprofit CEOs must be skilled at many activities unique to those organizations: identifying and securing financial resources, maintaining the organization's legitimacy, negotiating with other organizations, participating in various advocacy or political coalitions, and representing the organization's guiding principles. In most nonprofit organizations, the responsibility for handling these challenges falls directly on the CEO.

Therefore, nonprofit CEOs must have especially strong leadership abilities combined with specialized knowledge of their competitive arena. To complicate Carrie's challenge, replacing the founding CEO in any organization is a daunting task. In part, that is because no one can fully assume the founder's leadership role. The person can only *replace* the founder. And to replace the strong presence of a founding CEO, the new executive must quickly demonstrate the ability to influence others in the organization to acquire their confidence.

Carrie's most immediate challenges include attempting to promote some sense of stability during an unexpected period of transition and at the same time direct an effective transition process. To accomplish this, she will need to draw heavily upon staff members as well as board members to help her. She must quickly put together a competent transition team, which can ensure undisrupted leadership and management functions at each level as the CEO departs. The transition team will also have to be very involved in the recruitment, selection, and orientation of the new CEO.

Two important executives have expressed interest in the position, so Carrie must handle them carefully. Both will need to know as soon as practical that they are not going to be chosen and why. That will require delicate and genuine discussions between Carrie and each individual. As part of those discussions, Carrie should consider inviting them to serve on the transition team. If she can make them understand why they are not a good match for the position and how important they are to a smooth transition, she may gain their support.

Carrie has to clearly define what knowledge, skills, and abilities the replacement must possess before undertaking the recruitment process. She may decide to use a professional recruiting firm in identifying and screening qualified candidates for the position. Part of the preparation before recruitment will be to clarify the core values of the organization and the characteristics of the new CEO, who must lead the non-profit into the future. For this reason, the new CEO should have previously performed at or very near this level of responsibility.

A clear communication plan to let stakeholders, donors, and institutional funders know what is happening during the transition must also be developed. Without such a plan, rumours and miscommunications may spread. The transition team will need to include a primary communications officer. All internal and external communications must be coordinated by that person, who should report directly to Carrie and the transition team to ensure that a unified and consistent message is communicated.

In order to provide the level of support the new CEO will need in the early going, the selection should be a unanimous choice by the board, the transition team, and of course Carrie. But replacing a well-respected and highly successful leader will require more than agreeing on the new hire's qualifications. It will require genuine support for the replacement from all concerned. People only become leaders when others develop respect for their value, and that cannot be automatically assumed upon their arrival. But in the interim, until the new leader *earns* the genuine leadership role, everyone should do all they can to assist in the process.

If possible, Carrie should serve in a limited advisory role for a certain period after the new CEO arrives. If she is able to turn over the authority and decision making functions to this person but at the same time consult on critical matters, the likelihood of a successful transition will be increased significantly. Coming into the office after the new CEO begins may send conflicting signals about her role, but it will still be important for her to confer regularly with the new CEO for some reasonable length of time.

END NOTES

1   James Moschgat, "Leadership and the Janitor," *On Patrol Magazine,* Fall 2010, http://usoonpatrol.org/archives/2010/09/07/leadership-and-the-janitor.

2   John C. Maxwell and Jim Dornan, *Becoming a Person of Influence* (Nashville, TN: Maxwell Motivation, 1997).

3   Wayne Bodle, *The Valley Forge Winter: Civilians and Soldiers in War* (State College: The Pennsylvania State University Press, 2004).

4   George Orwell, *A Collection of Essays* (Orlando, FL: Houghton Mifflin Harcourt, 1981).

5   Tony Dungy and Nathan Whitaker, *Uncommon: Finding Your Path to Significance* (Carol Stream, Illinois Tyndale House Publishing 2011).

6   Arthur B. Laffer, "Reaganomics: What We Learned," *Wall Street Journal,* February 10, 2011.

7   Dorothy Herrmann, *Helen Keller: A Life* (Chicago: University of Chicago Press, 1998).

8   David Hardiman, *Ghandi: In His Time and Ours* (New York: Columbia University Press, 2003).

9   The Martin Luther King Papers Project: Farewell Statement for All India Radio, New Delhi, India, March 9, 1959.

10   John Y. Simon and Michael E. Stevens, *New Perspectives on the Civil War: Myths and Realities of the National Conflict* (Lanham, MD: Rowman & Littlefield, 2002).

11   Lewis R. Harlan and Raymond W. Smock, *The Booker T. Washington Papers, Volume 10: 1909-1911* (Urbana: University of Illinois Press, 1981).

12   Emory M. Thomas, *Robert E. Lee: A Biography* (New York: W.W. Norton & Company, 1995).

13 James Taranto and Leonard Leo, *Presidential Leadership: Rating the Best and the Worst in the White House* (New York: Wall Street Journal Books, 2004).

14 Douglas Keay, "No Such Thing as Society," *Woman's Own Magazine*, September 1987, http://briandeer.com/social/thatcher-societyhtm.

15 Dinesh D'Souza, *Ronald Reagan: How an Ordinary Man Became an Extraordinary Leader* (New York: Simon & Schuster, 1997).

16 Peter Robinson, "Tear Down this Wall: How Top Advisors Opposed Reagan's Challenge to Gorbachev—But Lost," *Prologue Magazine*, Summer 2007, http://www.archives.gov/publications/prologue/2007/summer/berlin.html.

17 David Greenberg, "Rewinding the Kennedy-Nixon Debates," *Slate Magazine*, September 2012, http://www.slate.com/articles/news_and_politics/history_lesson/2010/09/rewinding_the_kennedynixon_debates.html.

18 Bruce E. Winston and Kathleen Patterson, "An Integrative Definition of Leadership," *International Journal of Leadership Studies* 1, no. 3 (2006), http://www.regent.edu/acad/global/publications/ijls/new/vol1iss2/winston_patterson.doc/winston_patterson.htm.

19 R. M. Stogdill and A. E. Coons, *Leader Behavior: Its Description and Measurement* (Columbus: Bureau of Business Research, Ohio State University, 1957).

20 Rensis Likert, *New Patterns of Management* (New York: McGraw-Hill, 1961).

21 Travis Bradberry and Jean Greaves, *Leadership 2.0* (San Diego: Talent Smart, 2012).

22 Steven R. Covey, *The 7 Habits of Highly Effective People* (New York: Simon & Schuster, 2004).

23 Tim Tebow and Nathan Whitaker, *Through My Eyes* (New York: Harper Collins, 2011).

24 Fred Fiedler, *A Theory of Leadership Effectiveness* (New York: McGraw-Hill, 1967).

25 Paul Hersey, Kenneth Blanchard, and Dewey Johnson, *Management of Organizational Behavior: Leading Human Resources* (New York: Prentice Hall, 2007).

[26] Ken Blanchard and Patricia Zigarmi, *Leadership and the One Minute Manager* (New York: William Morrow & Company, 1985).

[27] Chad Brooks, "What Are Leadership Styles and Skills?," *Business News Daily*, June 2012, http://www.businessnewsdaily.com/2704-leadership.html.

[28] Emily Sohn, "Language Learning Begins in the Womb," *Discovery News*, January 2013, http://news.discovery.com/human/language-learning-begins-before-birth-130103.htm.

[29] Daniel Kahneman, *Thinking Fast and Slow* (New York: Farrar, Straus and Giroux, 2011).

[30] Coue, Emile. *Self Mastery through Conscious Autosuggestion*. Stilwell, KS: Digireads.com Publishing, 2006.

[31] Donald L. Kirkpatrick and James D. Kirkpatrick, *Evaluating Training Programs: The Four Levels* (San Francisco: Berrett & Koehler, 2006).

[32] Steve Smith, *Mentoring Can Build Great Leaders: If They Can Handle the Truth* (Lincoln: Office of University Communications, University of Nebraska, 2006).

[33] R. R. Blake and J. S. Mouton, *The Managerial Grid* (Houston: Gulf Publishing, 1964).

[34] Alan Axelrod, *Patton: A Biography* (New York: Palgrave Macmillan, 2005).

[35] David D. Burns, "The Perfectionist's Script for Self-Defeat," Psychology Today, November 1980, 53-67.

[36] Jerry Stocking, *Cognitive Harmony: An Adventure in Mental Fitness* (Chetek, WI: Moosehead Press, 1987).

[37] John P. Kotter, "What Leaders Really Do," *Harvard Business Review,* December 2001, 42-57.

[38] MindWorks Resources, "3 Primary Learning Modalities Everyone Uses," http://www.mindworksresources.com/p-324-3-primary-learning-modalities-every-person-uses.aspx.

[39] Kathy Condone, *Face-to-Face Networking: It's All About Communication* (Vancouver, WA: Kathy Condone, 2009).

[40] Albert Mehrabian, *Silent Messages; Implicit Communication of Emotions and Attitudes* (Belmont, CA: Wadsworth, 1981).

41 J. P. Doh, "Can Leadership Be Taught? Perspectives from Management Educators," *Academy of Management Learning and Education* 2, no. 1 (2003), 54-67.

42 Daniel G. Amen, *Change Your Brain: Change Your Life* (New York: Three Rivers Press, 1998).

43 Gary Yukl, *Leadership in Organizations*, 6th ed. (Upper Saddle River, NJ: Pearson, Prentice Hall, 2006).

44 Eugene Jennings, *The Mobile Manager* (New York: McGraw-Hill, 1971).

45 R. R. Blake and J. S. Mouton, *The Managerial Grid* (Houston: Gulf Publishing, 1964).

46 V. H. Vroom, *Work and Motivation* (New York: John Wiley & Sons, 1976).

47 V. H. Vroom and P. W. Yetton, *Leadership and Decision Making* (Pittsburgh: Pittsburgh University Press, 1976).

48 Barry Silverstein, *Motivation: Bringing Out the Best in Your People* (New York: Harper Collins, 2007).

49 Robert M. Guion and Scott Highhouse, *Essentials of Personnel Assessment and Selection* (New York: Routledge, 2006).

50 Diane Arthur, *Recruiting, Interviewing, Selecting, and Orienting New Employees* (New York: AMACOM, 2012).

51 Elizabeth Lloyd Mayer, *Extraordinary Knowing: Science, Skepticism, and the Inexplicable Powers of the Human Mind* (New York: Bantam Dell, 2007).

52 David P. Jones, *The Million Dollar Hire: Build Your Bottom Line One Employee at a Time* (San Francisco: Jossey-Bass, 2011).

53 Diane Arthur, *Workplace Testing: An Employers Guide to Policies and Practices* (New York: AMACOM, 1994).

54 Morris Massey, *The People Puzzle: Understanding Yourself and Others* (New York: Brady, 1979).

55 John H. Zenger and Joseph Folkman, *The Extraordinary Leader: Turning Good Managers into Great Leaders* (New York: McGraw-Hill, 2002).

56 Brayton R. Bowen, *Recognizing and Rewarding Employees* (New York: McGraw-Hill, 2000).

57 John P. Wanous, *Organizational Entry: Recruitment, Selection, Orientation, and Socialization of Newcomers* (New York: Prentice Hall, 1991).

58 Thomas J. Peters and Robert H. Waterman, *In Search of Excellence* (New York: Harper Collins, 1982).

59 Lewis R. Harlan, *Booker T. Washington: The Wizard of Tuskegee, 1901-1915* (New York: Oxford University Press, 1986).

60 David McCullough, *Truman* (New York: Simon & Schuster, 1992).

61 Robert H. Ferrell, ed., *The Autobiography of Harry S. Truman* (Columbia: University of Missouri Press, 1980).

62 Isaacson, Walter, Steve Jobs (New York, NY: Simon & Schuster, 2001).

63 Phillip Smith, ed., *The Autobiography of Benjamin Franklin* (New York: Dover Publications, 1996).

64 Walter Isaacson, *Benjamin Franklin: An American Life* (New York: Simon & Schuster, 2003).

65 Elizabeth Brown Pryor, *Clara Barton: Professional Angel* (Philadelphia: University of Pennsylvania Press, 1987).

66 David H. Burton, *Clara Barton: In the Service of Humanity* (New York: ABC-Clio, 1995).

67 James Berger, ed., *Helen Keller—The Story of My Life: The Restored Edition* (New York: The Modern Library, 2004).

68 Jay Matthews, *Escalante: The Best Teacher in America* (New York: Henry Holt & Company, 1988).

69 James B. Stewart, "The Real Heroes Are Dead," *The New Yorker*, February 2002, http://www.newyorker.com/archive/2002/02/11/020211fa_fact_stewart

70 Jacob Needleman, *Tao Ti Ching: Lao Tsu* (New York: Random House, 1997).

71 Robert K. Greenleaf, *Servant Leadership: A Journey into the Nature of Legitimate Power & Greatness* (Mahwah, NJ: Paulist Press, 1977).

72 Kent M. Keith, *The Case for Servant Leadership* (Westfield, IN: The Greenleaf Center for Servant Leadership, 2008).

73 Edwin A. Locke and Gary P. Latham, "Building a Practically Useful Theory of Goal Setting and Task Motivation: A 35-Year Odyssey," *The American Psychologist,* September 2002, 705-717.

74 Napoleon Hill, *Think and Grow Rich* (New York, NY: Success Books Company, 2009).

75 Phillippa Lally, Cornelia van Jarswaald, H. W. W. Potts, and J. Wardle, "How Habits are Formed: Modelling Habit Formation in the Real World," *European Journal of Social Psychology,* July 2009, http://onlinelibrary.wiley.com/doi/10.1002/ejsp.674/abstract.

INDEX

W

U

V

www.ingramcontent.com/pod-product-compliance
Lightning Source LLC
Chambersburg PA
CBHW030924180526
45163CB00002B/456